Teaching in Further Education

Trevor Kerry and Janice Tollitt-Evans

BLACKWELL
Oxford UK & Cambridge USA

© Trevor Kerry and Janice Tollitt-Evans 1992

The right of Trevor Kerry and Janice Tollitt-Evans to be identified as authors of this work has been asserted in accordance with the Copyright, Designs and Patents Act 1988.

First published 1992

Blackwell Publishers
108 Cowley Road
Oxford OX4 1JF
UK

Three Cambridge Center
Cambridge, Massachusetts 02142
USA

A CIP catalogue record for this book is available from the British Library.

Library of Congress Cataloging in Publication Data

Kerry, Trevor.
   Teaching in further education/Trevor Kerry and Janice Tollitt
-Evans.
      p. cm.
   Includes bibliographical references and index.
   ISBN 0–631–18127–X
   1. Adult education teachers—Training of—Great Britain.
2. Teaching—Handbooks, manuals, etc.   I. Tollitt-Evans, Janice,
1959–   II. Title.
LC5225.T4K47   1992
374'.007–dc20   91–39212
                                                                          CIP

Typset in 10 on 12pt Sabon
by TecSet Ltd

Printed in Great Britain

This book is printed on acid-free paper.

Contents

Index of Tasks

Index of Tables

Index of Figures

Acknowledgements

We wish to put on record our thanks to Carolle Kerry for her part in typing sections of this book and for undertaking the task of compiling the index, and to Maree Houghton for typing the remainder of the manuscript. Carolle and Alan, our respective spouses, were continuously tolerant of the time we gave to this project. We would like to thank Maria Blair who contributed information, and Joni Cunningham, advisory teacher for Further Education in Norfolk LEA, for reading the final draft; though we take full responsibility for any imperfections and inaccuracies in the text. The photograph of Janice Tollitt-Evans was taken by Adrian Kerry LBIPP, and that of Trevor Kerry by Alan Howard.

All known references and sources have been acknowledged. If we have inadvertently failed to acknowledge any source we invite notification and we apologize in advance.

INTRODUCTION

This is a book about teaching in Further Education. It is aimed at tutors who have come into FE from the professions with no formal training or background in teaching. Those who follow the CG 7307 course of initial training or proceed to the Cert.Ed.(FE) may find that it serves to amplify their training course. The book may also help train teachers who are coming into the FE sector for the first time, instructors undertaking YT training, and the many adult-education tutors who lack initial teacher training or sufficient ongoing in-service work. There may be other groups of trainers and leaders in sixth forms, in the Youth Service, in factories and training departments, who would benefit from at least some of the advice given here.

We hope this is a distinctive book. Our view is that it is distinctive in three ways.

First, this is a task book. It invites the reader to increase his or her awareness of professional skills, to work on those skills through seventy-five practical exercises or tasks, and thus to improve the skills in a conscious and systematic way. This kind of reader-involvement, awareness-raising and professional self-development activity is not wholly new. But it is unusual to find these methods applied to teaching skills at the Further Education level.

The second distinctive feature of this book is that it makes frequent reference to research or to theoretical underpinning when considering and analysing practical teaching skills. There are precedents for this, of course, but rarely at the Further Education level. We have been struck by the paucity of skills-based materials for teachers of Further Education classes. Most of the practical literature for tutors of this age group is either dated or aimed more at particular courses and systems than at the generic skills of teaching.

Third, this is a book which tries actively to promulgate a particular view of teaching in the post-16 sector. This view is characterized by student-centredness in learning, by professionalism in teaching and by a consciousness of modern developments which nevertheless retain the traditional standards and values of the teaching profession.

If we have fulfilled our aims in putting together a task-based skills book for teachers of Further Education, then there are some things which the reader should expect to find on the pages that follow and some which he or she should not. We hope that there will be no jargon. We have tried to avoid the trap of compiling sample lessons for direct implantation into your own classroom (most ready-made lessons will be inappropriate!). We have not been prescriptive over teaching methods since there is no golden mean of behaviour applicable to all post-16 classrooms in all circumstances. Nor is there such a thing as a perfect lesson.

Instead, we have attempted to isolate some key skills and issues in post-16 education. The book is divided into Units, each Unit focusing on a major theme and its related sub-themes. The Units are self-contained for the sake of clarity, but are often interrelated or cross-referenced since teaching skills operate in a context of varying human behaviour, not as isolated and mechanical phenomena. Within each Unit there are tasks for the reader to carry out either in his or her own classroom as the opportunity arises, or during a period of conscious teaching experimentation. Sometimes the tasks require the assistance of fellow professionals. This is because for too long, teaching has been a relatively private or autonomous activity whereas true professional development requires the sharing of others' wisdom and the contribution of one's own. The text is confined to fairly short blocks wherever possible, and much information is tabulated: there are fifty Tables and figures as well as numerous lists of salient information or questions. Our hope is that this layout will permit busy tutors to use the book selectively to fulfil their personal needs, and to utilize sections of it in an already busy professional programme; for, above all, this book is task-orientated. To read the volume from cover to cover would serve some purpose, but the true value lies in carrying out the tasks and reflecting on them.

We have collected references at the back of the book. In this way they leave the text uncluttered but are there for those who may wish to follow up specific topics as and when the need arises. It is particularly important for tutors to sharpen their minds on occasion by deliberate study of their own.

The psychologist B F Skinner once described education as 'what survives when what has been learned has been forgotten'. This book is offered in that spirit: the wisdom you acquire for completing the tasks should outlast the information printed on these pages. In this way you will have become the agent of your own professional advancement.

Unit 1

HANDLING RELATIONSHIPS WITH STUDENTS

Student expectations

If you were to take a group of FE students chosen at random and ask them why they had elected to undertake post-16 studies in an FE college, here is a typical range of replies you would receive:

'I want to get a qualification to get a (better) job.'

'I was fed up with being a kid at school.'

'You can study without all those awful GCSE exams.'

'Going to college means I have more independence.'

'My sister came here and she enjoyed it.'

'You get experience of real jobs.'

'You get more choice here.'

'They have all the right equipment so you get better experience.'

'At school they boss you around, here you can do what you want to.'

Hotstuff College, in its glossy prospectus, might of course put those sentiments in more sophisticated language . . . something like this, perhaps:

> At Hotstuff College you can choose from a wide range of vocationally orientated courses which will qualify you to compete successfully for a place in the world of work. You will be a student, with all that this implies for being responsible for meeting deadlines for course work and for studying alone at, or outside, college. Your tutors will be practitioners from the area of work you are studying for. They will not only teach you the knowledge and skills you will need, but will be there to give vocational advice. There are well-equipped simulated-work environments in the college, and you will spend some of your course on work placement. Most of your course will be monitored through continuous assessment . . . .

The point of these views and quotation is simply this: students will have particular *expectations* of a college, its atmosphere and ethos, its workings and, above all, the way in which the relationships between staff and students function. Perhaps the most fundamental skill for all FE staff is to establish the right tone of, and context for, those relationships.

Tutor–student relationships

Perhaps a good way to explore this issue would be for you to begin to look at your own relationships with students. The following Task might help you to make a start on this process.

Task 1   Examining your reactions to classroom events

How do you/would you react in each of the following situations? (Be honest; and if possible relate these examples to similar real situations you have experienced.) What would you do next?

1   Ten minutes after your class begins a student arrives and sits down in his/her place without explanation.
2   While the class is engaged on a written task you notice a normally lively girl student crying quietly to herself.
3   For the third time in a month a student fails to meet the deadline for a piece of course work.
4   The whole class has performed badly on a crucial piece of written work.

5   The group is about to go on a visit to a prestigious local company. Two minutes before you are due to set off one member of the group turns up with a newly acquired green Mohican hairdo.

6   Some of the students want to campaign for a vegetarian-only section in the canteen and wish to enlist your support.

7   The class finds a piece of work you have set in private study particularly difficult. You return from lunch to find them staging a 'sit-in' in the base-room and refusing to attempt it.

When you have completed Task 1 look back over all your responses. Estimate where you would come on the following continua:

Authoritarian	_____	Democratic
Humourless	_____	Humorous
Intolerant	_____	Tolerant
Formal	_____	Informal

The incidents described in Task 1 all put to the test the relationship between tutors and students. There are no absolute right answers as to how to behave in these situations: indeed, a good deal would depend on contextual factors which are not given. But the issues raised by these incidents help us to formulate the fundamental question about relationships:

To what ends are effective tutor–student relationships directed? Our view about this is that they are about helping students to become established as sensitive adults themselves, able to sustain good relationships of their own with those in authority and with peers; and eventually to become leaders themselves in their own private and working lives. Young people at the FE stage are often quite affected by role-models; and while these are not likely to be confined to college or vocational contexts they will, at this stage of their development, be acquiring crucial skills through the relationships and experiences.

Students' learning from relationships in college

So what kind of skills will students learn from their relationships with tutors and from the ethos of their course, and how will they learn them?

Obviously, one cluster of skills will centre around what might loosely be called 'appropriate behaviour'. If one looks at the work setting we could perhaps subdivide this into sub-skills; for example:

- safe practice for self and others
- respect for those in authority
- sensitivity towards peers
- helpfulness towards clients.

Again, in a vocational context, another cluster of skills might reflect aspects of 'discipline and self-discipline'. These skills, too, could be subdivided:

- punctuality
- dress-sense
- orderliness
- time management
- professional behaviour (etc.).

The ethos of the student's course and the nature of his/her relationships with tutors will convey messages about these skills and sub-skills. Part of the success of a good tutor is the degree to which these messages can be interwoven into the everyday life of the course so that they can be absorbed by students as part of the college culture rather than taught in any didactic way. It is appropriate, then, to pause here to think about what you think needs to be achieved and how you believe you can achieve it. To this end, try Task 2.

Task 2   Identifying relationship skills for students and how to achieve them through tutor–student relationships

1   Using the starting points of skills and sub-skills given in the text, try to identify the relationship skills *you* want *your* students to acquire. List them on the left-hand side of the page as in the example below:
    discipline and self-discipline:
    punctuality
    dress-sense
    orderliness
    time management
    professional behaviour.
    (You can, of course, add skills and sub-skills not listed in this Unit.)

2   Having listed your desired skills and sub-skills, use the right-hand column to indicate how you would try to achieve these ends through the ethos of your course and the relationships you yourself establish.

3   You may care to share these thoughts with your course-team of tutors. Do they
    - agree with your analysis of desirable skills?
    - agree with your proposed means to achieve them?

4   As a group, how successful do you feel you are already? If you are falling short on any item try to identify why, and what could be done about it.

Characteristics of a good FE tutor

A good FE tutor will be . . .

- fair
- professional
- knowledgeable in his/her subject
- confident
- a good listener
- friendly
- humorous
- able to share a joke
- a good practitioner in the work situation
- a well-balanced personality
- decisive
- well organized
- consistent
- able to deal with students as individuals
- a facilitator
- willing to spend time
- open to ideas and suggestions
- flexible
- approachable.

Contracts as part of a relationship

So far we have looked at the way in which the tutor–student relationships in an FE college tend to affect the learning-outcomes of students about appropriate relationships and behaviours. It is worth mentioning here something which seems rather obvious: that relationships are reciprocal. With this in mind it might be an opportune moment to draw attention to a useful tool in establishing tutor–student relationships in FE: the contract. Contracts will already be familiar to students from school through their Record of Achievement and the procedures associated with this. Contracts can be employed in various ways, and are probably at their most effective when they are quite informal, but still observed with care, e.g.

the tutor	*the students*
makes a point of being punctual at the beginning of classes, and ending on time	are expected always to be punctual unless there is a good reason for lateness
is always polite in addressing students and is never sarcastic	are polite to the tutor and their peers
consults students about, and explains the reasons for, regulations about dress.	accept responsibility for correct safety and wear sensible clothing for work placement.

They can be more formal, even written down, and at their extreme may be part of a disciplinary situation. For example, a tutor may give notice of exclusion to a student for failing to sustain attendance/course work/adequate standards subject to a quite formal contract that the student will attend on a specific number of occasions, keep specified deadlines or achieve a particular minimum standard. Contracts are generally viewed by students as 'fair', i.e., everyone knows where they stand and agrees to abide by the terms: which is precisely what happens in society. This concept of fairness is one which most FE students would list in a description of a good tutor. You may care to try Task 3, and then to compare your results with the list on page 7.

Task 3   Exploring with students what makes a good FE tutor

1   At an opportune moment ask each member of one or more of the classes you teach to list ten characteristics of a good FE tutor.
2   In a quiet moment go through the lists (there will be many items that recur). Make one list, with the recurrent items at the top (in order of frequency), and with the items that occur only once at the bottom.
3   Compare your list with the one on page 7.
4   How do you think you measure up to these 'ideal' pictures?

Establishing relationships

Finally, in this Unit we shall look at the process of establishing relationships in the FE class. Clearly, all relationships built on trust take time to develop, time so that the parties can get to know one another, can test one another's reliability and can build up feelings of confidence and security. But early on in the life of a class – at the beginning of an academic year, or when a class first forms partway through a year – the tutor needs to be aware of setting the context for that relationship to develop.

Teaching is an art or a science which is dependent not least on the 'chemistry' that operates between and within individuals and groups. First encounters can be critical in setting the tone; but these first encounters also need to be built on consciously over time. Different teachers will use different approaches and each may work successfully with some groups, or perhaps fail with others.

Time spent on thinking out first encounters with new groups of students may be a good investment. Consider these opening lines and their possible effectiveness:

'Let's get the admin out of the way first.'

'My name is Jane Smith. I thought we might all begin by joining in an ice-breaker game.'

'I would like to set out the ground rules early in the course.'

'Let's go round the group and each introduce ourselves.'

'Write me a big label to put on your desk so I get to know your names.'

'You look a keen group.'

'We're not going to learn anything today, we're going to find our way round the department.'

'Before we do ANYTHING else, we're going to learn the safety rules.'

'Welcome to your base-room: it's your home for the next two years.'

'The boy in the grey shirt, will you give out these syllabuses.'

So how would you handle the first encounter with a new class with a view to establishing good relations with all students? Task 4 gives you a chance to reflect on this.

Task 4   Handling first encounters

1   Choose one or two colleagues you know well and respect. Ask them how
     they handle first encounters:
     • What do they do to prepare before the day?
     • What do they do on the day?
     • What do they do when they do meet the class?
2   Reflect on any encounters of your own:
     • What did you do badly?
     • What did you do well?
     • What did you learn?
3   Plan your next 'first encounter'. Write down the plan. Keep a record of what
     actually happens. Compare the two after the event.

Conclusion

This chapter has been about tutor–student relationships. We started with these
because they are central to everything else that happens in the class. In the next
Unit we move on to a related topic: the way in which personal and social
development of students can be catered for.

Unit 2

HELPING PERSONAL AND SOCIAL DEVELOPMENT

The role of personal tutor

The role of the personal tutor has been well established for a number of years in Further Education. This role is distinct and quite separate from that of course or subject tutor, although many tutors from choice or necessity adopt a dual role. It has become an increasingly diversified role as it has evolved, and is now an extremely responsible position to hold, as the following list of functions illustrates.

The personal tutor should:

- ensure a structured induction programme for each student
- work with students on a group and individual basis
- timetable individual contact on a regular basis
- timetable and monitor group contact
- work with the college careers officer and course tutor to make sure the students receive a structured careers education programme, to include individual interviews with the careers officer (see Unit 12)
- work with the course tutor to ensure that a quality work experience programme is arranged which is appropriate to each student's needs and which offers progression
- work with the student to develop action plans, a curriculum vitae and Records of Achievement in a way which conforms to national standards
- work with the college welfare officer in cases of referral when problems arise which require help from other internal or external agencies

- work with the course tutor and other members of the course team and placement supervisors to monitor and evaluate the student's academic progress and practical skills
- work with other team members to ensure the delivery of a health education programme and health and safety policy which cuts across all subject areas (to include provision of a health education resource bank and provision of an optional/compulsory course in basic first aid).

The list of typical responsibilities of a personal tutor may suggest that a personal tutor's main concern is to enhance the quality of learning and help students work towards the appropriate career. But equally important is helping the student find a path through life.

Personal tutors need to be aware of these wider concerns when working closely with young people, for they are in the formative process of shaping their futures: not only in terms of employment, higher education or further training, but in terms of adopting a particular lifestyle.

At this stage in their lives some students are involved in a considerable process of change which may include one or more of the following:

- leaving the locality of birth
- moving away from family and established friends
- managing their own financial affairs
- living in a new kind of community
- decision-making and goal-setting without parental help
- accessing unprecedented levels of freedom
- making long-term career decisions
- seeking employment.

Developing the personal tutor role

Your role as a personal tutor might follow through a sequence related to the academic year. This might begin thus:

- liaison with high schools
- initial advice and guidance
- enrolment
- induction
- tutoring.

Tutoring involves a great deal of liaison: with the careers officer, student welfare officer, course team members and sometimes, outside agencies. Table 1 illustrates this and shows how the development of common skills, health education and dealing with students' individual problems are predominant.

TABLE 1   The developing role of the personal tutor and its context

Personnel	Functions
Personal tutor	Induction Setting up and monitoring work experience Individual/group tutorials, timetables and development of common skills Awareness of health education Dealing with individual problems as and when they occur Referral to outside agencies/college/student welfare officer – e.g. for drugs, pregnancy-related problems, etc. Development of action plans Development of records of achievement Development of CVs and application procedures Development of work experience logbooks and student contracts.
Careers officer	Individual and group careers interviews and tutorials Liaison with higher-education staff/employers on students' behalf.
Course team	Development of course skills Awareness of health education Dealing with individual academic problems (as and when they arise).
Student welfare officer	Dealing with individual problems Referral to outside agencies when necessary – e.g. health problems related to pregnancy, drug abuse, medical conditions, e.g. HIV+.

Again, Table 1 is a convenient means of summarizing aspects of the personal tutor's role, but it may lead you to think that the personal and social development of students is all very direct and intentional, whereas much of the work in this area is done *indirectly*. Young people develop in so many different ways over a period of time, longer than that covered by a college course, and may be profoundly affected by the 'hidden curriculum'. Personalities play a large part in this development: yours, the students' and those of other teachers. Students give different impressions of themselves and their abilities to different members of staff. Therefore, a combined approach must be employed in order to see the 'whole picture', the 'whole person'. For example, as a teacher of information technology, you may feel that a particular student is very shy and lacking in confidence. But this may be a reaction to a subject area he/she feels very unsure about. The student may be confident and assertive when working with a different teacher of a subject in which he/she is competent.

Some courses have the "combined approach" built into the course assessment scheme. This is true of BTEC courses and, increasingly, of 'A' level programmes. Course team members meet to assess students over a wide range of 'common skills' shown over a period of time and through different activities, e.g. group work, assignments, individual presentations, etc. This helps to provide a well-balanced view and assessment of each student. Strengths and weaknesses brought to light in such assessments can then be discussed and worked on with individual students in tutorial.

Other courses may not contain or demand such a systematic tutorial component; for example, part-time courses, a GCE 'A' level matrix or a college certificate programme. Where personal tutoring is not a required component of course structure, extra care must be taken by tutors to ensure that students receive the skills they need to acquire and any help they may desire.

Some colleges identify all staff as personal tutors to a group of students; those staff who are less at ease with this role are in special need of professional development to help them understand and cope. For some institutions personal tutoring is available, but mainly 'on demand'. In other words, the student has actively to seek help. This may inhibit the more timid, despite real need. Some colleges provide a specialist counselling service, but personal tutoring, with its emphasis on immediate support and encouragement of life skills, should not be compared with the specialized functions of counsellors.

The personal tutor may find it especially helpful to liaise with placement supervisors.

Placement reports provide some relevant information regarding personal and social development, but visits will be necessary to obtain detailed information about how the experience has highlighted strengths and weaknesses which are not covered by written reports. This information could range from the student's manner with clients/children/patients etc., to 'mixing' with placement personnel (e.g. does the student mix with other staff at break-times and lunch-time comfortably?). This type of social ease is a necessary part of the world of work and should not be ignored. If students find it difficult to communicate with people of different age-groups or in positions of responsibility it shows an area of concern which could be worked on in college.

Placement personnel are in the unique position of seeing your students in the workplace on a day-to-day basis, often working alongside them on shared tasks. They therefore have many opportunities to observe students and assess them not only during working hours, but also in more unguarded moments at recreation times. The placement contribution is therefore extremely valuable, especially if the placement is the type of employment the student hopes to proceed to after training. In certain extreme cases, placement supervisors may feel the student to be totally unsuited to the job and the personal tutor's task then may be to counsel the student very sensitively and carefully seek to help towards a major change of career direction.

This section was headed 'Developing the personal tutor role', so this may be an opportune moment to pause to take stock of your own skills. Use Task 5 to this end.

Task 5   Analysing your own skills as a personal tutor

Carry out a 'skills audit' of your own abilities as a personal tutor. The process is straightforward:

1   Visualize a group of students for whom you act as personal tutor.
2   List the strengths you believe you have in this role. Try to jot down what evidence you are using to identify these strengths.
3   Then list the skills you would like to develop further, or which you feel you lack.
4   Finally, try to suggest for yourself ways in which you can tackle the issues raised by your responses to the last item. Turn your thoughts into an action plan.

Towards independence

Independence is the goal towards which you are encouraging your students: to arm them with all the necessary skills and abilities needed in life and in the world of work.

Unit 9 deals in more detail with record-keeping and tracking progress. But here it is opportune to introduce the subject by saying that recording requires a broad approach which includes more than information about academic progress. As always, the best approach requires a degree of planning and structure. You will want to evolve your own structures, appropriate to your students and circumstances. Table 2 illustrates a possible approach for you to use to aid your thinking or to compare with any extant system which you use.

TABLE 2   Strategies and purposes for recording

Strategy	Purpose
Use of student logbooks	For students to jot notes in work-experience placements and in college sessions. Students can then assess for themselves knowledge acquired and skills and abilities developed, in addition to problems encountered and possible solutions.
Use of tutorials	In both individual and group mode to ensure optimum benefit for both the student and yourself.

This strategy involves the use of ongoing records of:

(a)   the student's contract – drawn up jointly to establish the baseline from which he/she will progress, expectations and commitment to deadlines for assignments, good attendance, etc.
(b)   your plans for the tutorial
(c)   the student's feedback on targets achieved and future goals to be set
(d)   strengths and weaknesses of the student and action plans made as a result
(e)   negotiation between yourself and the student on contract, assignments, etc.
(f)   any referrals to internal/external agencies.

Records of life-skills work, e.g. economic awareness	This can record cross-curricular information built into the syllabus and/or outside speakers presenting information, e.g. business managers or specialist advisers from the local education authority contributing to a series of seminars on how successful companies operate and why they are necessary to create the nation's wealth. Lessons learned from a work experience can be added. Information about sessions on, e.g., managing personal finances can be recorded.

Records of the kind described in Table 2 build towards a picture of the 'whole student' – a theme to which we return in Unit 9.

Postscript on giving advice

The personal tutor needs to be aware of, and realistic about, giving advice. Below are some statements about the advice given by personal tutors – the statements come from personal tutors themselves.

Task 6   Giving advice

Read each of the statements below. In each case try to recall an example from your own experience that would support the view expressed. Overall, what things does this exercise tell you about giving advice to students?

'My own experience of this situation is very limited.'

'My view is coloured by my personal bias.'

'Academic advice is easier to give than career guidance or personal help.'

'I know I can't, but I often want to be personally involved.'

'It is hard to be emotionally detached.'

'I'm only a sounding-board, an honest broker.'

'In the end, the decision belongs to the student, not to me.'

'I have no idea where to begin with this problem.'

'This information, given in confidence, may affect my judgements in future.'

'I feel more secure when I am helping other people.'

Task 7   Revisiting your personal tutor skills' action plan

Look back to the action plan you made as a result of Task 5. Do you wish to revise and update it in any way?

Unit 3

CREATING A LEARNING ENVIRONMENT

Becoming conscious of the physical environment

Most of us would probably agree that we work best in surroundings in which we feel comfortable: indeed, the DIY industry depends on us all being prepared, at regular intervals, to change or upgrade the environment we choose to live in.

The learning environment is probably dependent on more subtle factors than a new wallpaper design; and for this reason alone is worthy of more analytical attention. When we recall that students may spend between twenty and thirty hours a week in their learning-base or lecture rooms the issue of how conducive these are is certainly worthy of attention. In previous chapters it has been made clear that part of the creation of a learning environment is about the ethos of a college or course and the tutor–student and peer-group relationships that are engendered on it. But the physical environment and, more importantly, the messages this gives out, must be a factor in the satisfaction of students even if we have no direct control over the colour of the walls or the frequency of redecoration.

Consider the following contrasting descriptions of two real locations recently witnessed:

A science laboratory

> 'My first impression was of a rather down-at-heel traditionalism. But as I began to take in the details, the true awfulness of the

location began to dawn on me. The old-fashioned wooden benches and raised teacher's desk were unavoidable; and old wood has a friendly quality anyway. It was the clear evidence of carelessness that really hurt. There were cupboards – oak with glass fronts – to which sheaves of unused papers, faded envelope files, and torn, abandoned textbooks had been confined by generations of staff; a windowed dustbin of a cupboard put to no practical use. From the drawers of the students' benches there protruded the remnants of a thousand – more perhaps – illicit snacks: the crispbags and Mars wrappers of half a year almost out of sight, so effectively out of mind. The floors were swept and the surfaces polished; that was the cleaner's job. But on the teacher's desk sat a chemical balance with one scale pan missing and minus half the weights. The door of the desk cupboard hung half-open on a hinge that needed two twists of a screwdriver . . . .'

The base-room

'The notice on the outside of the door announced the identity of the occupants and said 'Welcome' in big letters. Inside, the furniture was laid out to allow access to all parts of the room through little gangways. The students had been working on physical development; and a grinning skeleton hung in a corner while the adjacent surfaces were filled with build-a-body models and Resusci dolls. On the walls behind were photographs, taken by the students, of children of various ages. The pictures were well displayed on coloured backgrounds with short, informative commentaries. On another wall was information about the charity collections the students had been engaged in recently. A third wall was shared between a stand holding a display of vocational magazines and a series of posters about health hazards in the workplace. Behind the teacher's desk on a white board, were the learning targets for this week's placement experience.'

Improving the physical environment

These two brief descriptive extracts could be replicated, for better or worse, across the country in FE institutions. It takes little imagination to conceive from the descriptions which learning environment students would find more conducive. Yet, as tutors, we are often reluctant to grasp this nettle, and much too ready to blame the maintenance programme, the government's parsimonious views on education, or the college management when we should be looking closer to home for solutions (or at least for improvements!). We mean, of course, to ourselves and our students.

With this in mind you might care to try Task 8. This asks you to have a really objective look around the learning environment which you work in – and which you have helped to create.

▶ Task 8   Looking at your own learning environment

(If you have a course base-room or a personal classroom use this for your analysis here; if not, work on the room you use most often.)

1   Begin by having a good look round the room, its layout and design. It may help to make a list of what its facilities are:
  • cupboards
  • furniture
  • wall-space
  • pin-boards etc.
2   Are these facilities used effectively? Go through the list and assess the situation, e.g.:
  • Is there clutter in the room?
  • Do the cupboards need reorganizing?
  • Is the furniture appropriately/flexibly arranged?
  • Is the wall space used to promote learning?
  • Is student work displayed?
  • Does the room mirror a vocational environment, or could it? etc.
3   Do you, and your students feel a pride – or at least an ownership – of the space?
4   How could you promote this sense of ownership
      for yourself?
      for students?
5   Systematically think out how the physical environment of the room could be used more effectively to promote and support learning and teaching.

Apart from the fundamental décor which may be beyond our control, each of us can and does have a profound influence on the learning environment in our classes. If our attitude to the learning environment is one of inertia, then our effect will not be neutral, but negative. It should be part of the basic professionalism of every teacher in any context or phase of education to have a positive effect – in collaboration with students – upon the learning environment which they all share. This is true not only of classroom or workshop space, but of tutorial environments, too.

A *checklist for the base room*

You might like to consider the use of each of the following actions to sustain or improve your learning environment. Some should be, or become, second nature; some you may choose to use somtimes or to reject. They are not listed in any putative order of importance. You may wish to add your own.

- Make a weekly rota of students responsible for upkeeping general tidiness.
- Tidy up every day before you leave.
- Change displays every two or three weeks.
- Always keep some student work on show.
- Make sure all equipment has a home and everyone knows and uses it.
- Have a termly clear-out.
- Be aware of safety: no trailing wires, etc.
- Make and agree simple rules to control litter, etc.
- Have a library/study corner.
- Keep administrative notices on boards.
- Don't pin up notices by one corner only.
- Avoid sellotape on walls.
- Have a 'Today' board for urgent information.
- Encourage visitors (e.g. work-placement providers).
- Beg or grow some pot-plants.
- When purchasing new items, have an eye to colour, design, stackability, etc.
- Keep the room aired.
- Even in workshops, keep everything clean.

Creating an intellectual environment

The physical environment for learning is important, as we have seen, and inevitably has an effect on student morale; but much of the improvement is not dependent on new plant and expensive furniture: it is the attitude and the approach on the part of both tutors and students which are most formative. But the intellectual environment of the classroom is also a factor in determining the effectiveness of a particular student group. Most students come to college because they want, above all, to obtain vocational qualifications. However, that should not narrow the focus of all thinking to a specific job or a small cluster of academic or practical subjects. The effective tutor will be anxious to make the class a forum within which much wider issues can be discussed, or opinions expressed. College is, to use the jargon, not only about training, but about education. Sometimes these broader discussions will be:

- tutor-initiated
- tutor-led
- tutor-dominated.

Often, in the right environment, they will be:

- student-initiated
- student-led
- tutor-free.

Let us be clear at this point precisely what is being described here, and what is not. This might best be illustrated by a series of vignettes of typical situations, each followed by a brief comment.

Vignette 1   In a staff meeting tutors have been discussing how to allocate classrooms to courses in the next session. When views have been received the deputy principal makes decisions based on all the factors involved. Tutor A does not like the outcome, and implies to students that their course is undervalued by the college management. Tutor A also feeds in typical newspaper articles on how demonstrations and sit-ins have altered management decisions in a local factory.

Comment   Tutor-initiated, tutor-led, but strictly taboo. College is not about political game-playing by students and it is not professional for young students, devoid of real insight into a given situation, to be made victims of the unwillingness of a member of staff to take the appropriate professional steps to air a grievance.

Vignette 2   In an NNEB course each week a student is delegated to scan the library copies of the Times Educational Supplement and similar papers and to photocopy any article about nursery nurses or children 0–5 years. The extracts are displayed on the 'Today' board in the room; and formal and informal discussion is encouraged.

Comment   Tutor-initiated but partly student-led. A useful kind of ongoing exercise. It creates good attitudes towards seeking, absorbing and assessing information about the profession.

Vignette 3   The largest local employer shuts down unexpectedly. Students bring in the local paper. Some of their parents are affected. Students are angry about what they see as injustices about the way the company has acted.

Comment   Student-initiated and student-led. Initially the reactions may be only emotional. With sympathetic handling, this whole scenario can be directed by the tutor into many different layers of learning, such as

- empathy with those affected
- relevance to their own future work situation
- in some cases, coping with changed family circumstances.

Vignette 4 Christmas is coming close. The class decides one lunch-time that it would like to put on a Christmas entertainment for the department. They organize themselves, according to inclination and ability, to prepare traditional fare, sing carols, tell a ghost story, recite poetry, read a Dickens extract and play traditional games.

Comment Student-initiated, student-led, and largely tutor-free. Nevertheless, a good social learning experience with a lot of 'intellectual' skills required too, in finding and performing suitable materials and understanding them in the process.

So the learning environment contains, we have suggested in the course of these three Units, four important elements:

- effective tutor–student relations
- sensitive peer-group social relations
- a well-organized physical environment
- an appropriate intellectual demand on students' education, not just training.

This is especially relevant in view of the recent government proposals for general NVQs.

An environment for study

Perhaps there should be one other aspect highlighted in the brief review of the ingredients of a good learning environment. This would be the skill of the tutor in creating study habits in the students, so our fifth dimension would be

- effective study skills.

The 1987 HMI survey *NAFE in practice* drew attention to the fact that nearly all FE students are expected to study in their own time – writing up practical work, going over mock exam questions, undertaking projects for continuous assessment, and so on. Much of this work was quite vital to the student's progress, and was often assessed. But HMI were drawn nevertheless to conclude that: 'The teaching of study skills is frequently neglected.' This is an unacceptable state of affairs and needs to be addressed. In NVQ courses, for example, such skills as those of communication are a requirement in the core skills element (see Unit 16). It might be useful to pause at this point to look at your own procedures for teaching study skills and for supporting students' private study.

Task 9   Looking at study skills and private-study provision

1   Does your college, department, course have a policy on teaching study skills? Are these policies written down? Can you find them? (It will be useful to do so.)

2   If there is a policy:
   • How effective is it?
   • Is it adhered to?
   • How could it be strengthened and improved?

3   If there is no policy:
   • Why not?
   • What could be done about it at department or course level?
   • What policy could you implement at course, or even class, level?

4   What do you think students need to learn about study skills? Why? How can these things best be communicated?

What precise study skills students need to know may vary to some extent in detail from course to course, but there is probably a core of skills that would be of value to the vast majority of students. Table 3 gives a kind of 'pick and mix' list: beginning from the items there you can

• select
• omit
• add
• vary the relative significance of any given item

but from it you can begin to build your own study skills scheme.

Task 10   Reviewing study skills for students

Compare your list of essential study skills generated in Task 9, no. 4, with the list in Table 3. Make any adjustments you think appropriate.

TABLE 3   Some study skills required by FE students

Most, if not all, students will need these abilities:

- to concentrate for reasonable periods
- to listen closely
- to take notes in a concise and readable form
- to write in a planned way
- to write in appropriate styles or formats
- to learn from visual materials, e.g. video
- to study alone
- to use a contents page
- to use an index
- to use a library catalogue
- to ask questions when things are unclear
- to work to a time-scale
- to plan practical work before starting
- to perform tasks neatly and clearly
- to learn from peers
- to reflect on and learn from practical experiences
- to plan a study programme
- to combat reasonable distractions
- to prioritize
- to lead a sensible life in term-time
- to articulate what they have learned
- to use a word-processor
- to judge their own levels of performance without supervision
- to know when to take a break or stop
- to interpret written (e.g. exam) questions
- to have access to language support if required.

The items listed in Table 3, augmented by you in Task 9, link directly to work for National Vocational Qualifications.

Provision for private study

Finally in this chapter it would be fitting to look at the provision which is made overall in college for students to study privately. Task 11 will help you to review private-study provision. Use the questions in it both to examine provision in your institution and to begin to formulate how you can maximize your use, through the work set and opportunities given to students, of the provision.

Task 11   Exploring private-study and resource-based learning provision in the college

1   What private-study facilities are provided in the college? (List what exists, adding categories of your own to those provided below to start you off):
   • library area
   • book/journal provision
   • video replay
   • computers/word-processors
   • help with literacy/numeracy problems
   • tutorial assistance available
   • other facilities (list them).

2   Now go back through your list, and for *each category* answer the following questions (it may help the review process if you write your responses down):
   • How adequate is the facility?
   • To what extent do you as a tutor liaise with those who need the facility?
   • How do you raise students' awareness of how, when and why to access the facility?

3   Look back over your review. What lessons does it contain for:
   • you
   • your students
   • your course/department *staff*
   • the institution?

4   How can you begin to put into action the issues identified above?

In these first three Units we have been trying to establish the relationship and environmental base from which effective learning can be achieved. In Unit 4 we move on to begin to examine essential skills for the tutor, beginning with curriculum planning.

Unit 4

PLANNING AND DOCUMENTING THE CURRICULUM

Introduction

Most full-time Further Education tutors will find themselves responsible for planning at least a section of the curriculum, and many take on the role of course planners for new course initiatives. Part-time tutors in Further Education and adult education, too, are increasingly involved in this process. Curriculum planning is, therefore, an essential skill for all tutors. But in these days when curriculum has not only to serve the needs of validating bodies, but is subject to scrutiny by employers, by advisers and inspectors, by students themselves through the media of marketing and evaluation and by college committees via performance indicators, this process of curriculum planning is inevitably linked to curriculum documentation.

It can be very daunting for a relatively new tutor, or one who is unfamiliar with this process, to be faced with the task of planning and documenting the whole or part of a new course curriculum, or updating an existing one. This Unit is designed to give you some basic skills of curriculum planning and documentation which you can build upon as you become more familiar with the process. We shall assume that the documentation takes the form of a course booklet – a booklet which can be used to tell both the students and the validating body (or others who may have a legitimate interest) as much as possible about the course. (In marketing your course you would use a précis from this larger body of information – see Unit 17.) We shall also assume that you are wanting to plan the course from new; but the process is equally suitable for revising existing material.

Elements in a curriculum plan

It is helpful to begin by knowing the kinds of things that need to go into a curriculum plan. Curriculum is a broad term, almost an elastic one. In the recent past curriculum was often confused with syllabus or content. But curriculum includes not only the knowledge-content of a course, but the whole range of educational experiences that together make up the total student experience of that course. Table 4 sets out the key elements for course planning and documentation.

 ## Task 12   Looking critically at your own course documentation

Study the list of twenty-five key elements in the generation of a documented curriculum as listed in Table 4. Using this list, scrutinize the documentation for one of the courses with which you are involved. Answer these questions:
- Does your documentation cover all these elements?
- If so, how well does it do so?
- If not, which are missing?
- Does your documentation suggest that any additional items should be added to the list?
- What are these?

TABLE 4   Twenty-five key elements in the generation of a documented curriculum

The tutor will need to consider and document each of the following:
- the purpose and rationale for the course
- the target group(s) at whom the course is aimed
- the overall aims and intentions of the course
- the entry requirements
- the need for the course and how this has been established
- the liaison processes, e.g. with local employers
- the consultation processes, e.g. in the college's committees
- the place of the course within the college/department 'portfolio'

- the validation process: stages and time-scales
- the staffing resource implications of the course and how they are to be met
- the financial implications of the course (equipment, materials)
- the physical resources required (accommodation)
- the management of the course
- the time allocations relating to staff, students and components of the course, including timetables
- the professional preparation and continuing development of tutors
- the course content: the syllabus, its component parts and their integration
- the common skills and core elements for the course
- the resultant student learning: competencies, skills, knowledge and understanding
- the practical aspects of learning, e.g. simulated work environments
- the work-placement requirements of the course
- the teaching and learning methods to be promoted in the curriculum
- the assessment methods to be used for each component, practical and theoretical
- the support, tutorial, profiling and reporting procedures of the course, including the commitment to equal opportunities
- the success criteria or performance indicators for the course
- the processes for monitoring, reviewing and evaluating the course.

A commentary on the twenty-five key elements in a documented curriculum

So far in this Unit you have looked at what validators, staff, students and employers need to know about a course, and you have compared this list with extract documentation of your own. We have suggested that all this information should be compiled into a course booklet. Some validating bodies require this; some have pre-determined formats to which tutors have to conform. Most such booklets would begin appropriately with introductory material about the college and department/faculty or school, and about such issues as its learning resources and library or computing provision. Mention would be made here, too, of overall college services available to students: a counselling service, student union facilities, catering provision, extracurricular activities available, and so on. All these things – along with intangibles such as college ethos – contribute to the 'hidden curriculum'. The 'hidden curriculum' is a vital ingredient in the total curriculum which is on offer to the student.

Having set out these curricular matters as a context, it is possible to move on more meaningfully to the more detailed elements already listed in Table 4. What we are going to do in this section is to take each element in turn and provide a brief commentary on it.

1   *The purpose and rationale for the course*
The rationale is a statement of the logical basis for the course and its curriculum and teaching and learning methods. It will include the course purposes, stated quite succinctly at this stage. Perhaps it would help you to think of it as the mission statement for the individual course, flowing out of broader institutional mission statements.

2   *The target groups at whom the course is aimed*
It is essential to spell these out, not least for marketing purposes. If the course is to be slanted at a specific group or groups – an age group, a gender audience with a specific skill/qualification, or with a particular deficiency – these need to be acknowledged.

3   *The overall aims and intentions of the course*
What is your course going to equip the students to do that they could not have done beforehand? The more clearly this can be stated, the more likely the course is to meet its target.

4   *The entry requirements*
These may be restrictive, or wholly open. Potential students need to know so as not to waste time applying unnecessarily.

5   *The need for the course and how this has been established*
This section probes the effectiveness of your research first among employers (or relevant others such as the placement providers), and then among potential consumers. Most college validating boards and nearly all external validators require documentary evidence on these issues.

6   *The liaison processes, e.g. with local employers*
In this section one should provide evidence that local employers have been consulted about the practical and theoretical aspects of the course content. Any necessary or useful consultative mechanisms, such as course committees, should be described – along with their pattern of meetings and terms of reference.

7   *The consultation process*
Each college will have its own set of standard practices, which should be adhered to and documented.

8   *The place of the course within the college/department 'portfolio'*
Courses which stand alone may be less successful than those which hold a logical niche in the total college provision. The logic of establishing this

particular course, at this specific level, should be explained and any concerns about duplication of provision dispelled.

9   *The validation process: stages and time-scales*
For planning new courses it is helpful to set out a timetable, leaving room for setbacks or contingencies. For ongoing courses, the documentation should explain the nature and frequency of revalidation requirements where these exist.

10   *The staffing resource implications of the course and how they are to be met*
Every course is a drain on resources: human, financial and material. Often new courses draw heavily on one or two members of staff with specific training or qualifications acquired with a view to that course being set up. One needs to reflect, here, on the implications of deploying staff to this course rather than another. Can all courses be adequately staffed, or must something else go? What are the implications of these decisions?

11   *The financial implications of the course (equipment, materials)*
Setting up a new course can be expensive as it may require resources not previously available. But new equipment will bring with it financial implications for the future: maintenance costs, the need to update and eventual replacement.

12   *The physical resources required (accommodation)*
It is tempting to ignore this category. But an effective pre-nursing course cannot be mounted in a derelict motor-vehicle workshop, nor a good vehicle-maintenance course in a classroom.

13   *The management of the course*
This section will set out who is to be course tutor, the responsibilities of subject or work-based tutors, the pattern of course team meetings and the mechanisms for continuing consultation with appropriate college boards or committees. The course management personnel, structures and processes need to be agreed *before* the course begins.

14   *The time allocations relating to staff, students and components of the course including timetables*
Here it is necessary to set out the detail of how staff will be deployed to the course, the mode of attendance and how students will divide their time between classroom, workshop and work placement. The extent and duration of individual subjects or activities need to be set out unambiguously. The most

effective way to do this for a new course is to draw up 'sample timetables', i.e. what would be happening in reality if the course were running. In this way plans can be checked for realism and flaws.

15   *The professional preparation and continuing development of tutors*
Often staff will need professional development before they are equipped to begin a new course. The documentation should indicate that this has been undertaken. It is important in this context to remember that professional development may include not merely attendance at courses or conferences, but focused visits to other colleges, or a placement in a relevant work-placement situation. But, even when the course is up and running, staff will need skills to be honed and updated; and a wide range of strategies should be deployed to achieve this.

16   *The course content: the syllabus, its component parts and their integration*
By now it will be obvious that course planning and documentation is a far more sophisticated process than simply compiling a syllabus. But the content is important in itself. It must be relevant, up to date and based on sound practice. Links between theory and practice need to be made. Within the whole syllabus are the component parts; not just subjects in the old-fashioned sense, but the areas of understanding which promote good learning. Thus, a syllabus on child care may have components about the law, about psychology, about the sociology of child development, about practical skills in the nursery, and so on. But the course content is more than the sum of the parts, and requires the compiler to articulate the points of integration between these sections and how, in the teaching and learning process, they are to be knitted together into a seamless whole. Each component's distinctive perspective is only one facet of a whole understanding.

17   *The common skills and core elements for the course*
It may be useful to begin by giving an extended quotation from a recent NCVQ report, a report which attempts to define core elements or skills:

> The term 'core skill' has been used in a variety of ways. This is illustrated in some detail in the recent report by Tim Oates.
> In the current NCVQ report, the primary core skills identified are those which underpin almost all performance, such as problem solving and communication. The essential point about these facets of competence, and that which is central to their inclusion in this report, is the extent to which the skills are *common* to behaviour in different areas and contexts. If the skills are common and widely

applicable, or some aspect of the skill is common, it is that common aspect that we are defining as 'core'. This is based upon the assumption that the acquisition of the core skill in some areas of competence and contexts offers the potential of generalisation or transfer to other areas and contexts which employ the same skill. We are therefore seeking to identify those aspects of skill which are common and transferable to a wide range of performance.

The concept of *transfer* is of course central to all education. One function of school education is presumably to equip young people with a range of skills, knowledge and understanding to prepare them for the problems they will meet in life and work as adults. The pursuit of an academic discipline such as History at A level is not simply to prepare people to become historians. Historians are valued as potential employees for a variety of diverse reasons including the breadth of vision and perspective brought about by studying in depth our civilisation and culture, and the 'set' of enabling skills developed within the rigours of a discipline, including the ability to analyse problems, sift information, weigh evidence, evaluate solutions and to communicate effectively. In essence it is believed the possession of these skills, developed to a high order, by for example, historians, can be applied to activities other than history. This is why employers are likely to value applicants with A level or degrees in History. To take another example, the pursuit of a scientific discipline develops research methodology which is another approach to problem solving having wide application beyond the discipline in which it is acquired.

The second type of core skills identified in the lists proposed are those which, although not fundamental to behaviour in the way described above, are nevertheless highly desirable and useful in a variety of situations. These currently include such 'skills' as a familiarity with information technology and competence in foreign languages. They are requirements of our time and would not have been in the list of core skills a hundred years ago. The first and second categories of core skills are not mutually exclusive, however, because information technology provides people with techniques and methodology that also have wide application. (Jessup 1990a)

Here it may be helpful for the reader to refer to Units 2 and 6 of this book, where more detail is given on this topic. There it will be seen that, using a 'spiral learning' method, the students will be able to develop common skills and gain information which increases in complexity throughout the course. Core themes and common skills will span the entire curriculum as follows:

Core themes	Common skills
Resources	Self-development
Environment	Learning and studying
Health and safety	Self-management and organization
Equal opportunities	Working with others
Human needs	Communicating
Development of the individual	Information seeking and analysis
Career development	Using information technology
	Numeracy
	Identifying/tackling problems
	Practical skills
	Science and technology
	Design skills

These need to be well integrated and carefully monitored to ensure that no omissions are made.

18   *The resultant student learning: competencies, skills, knowledge and understanding*
A syllabus or course content does not of itself produce appropriate abilities. First, it is useful for both teachers and learners, if learning intentions of the course are clearly articulated. Second (see no. 19), one needs to pay attention to the teaching and learning methods that will achieve these ends. Here we have used four descriptions about course outcomes which we would define as follows:

- competencies – the routine abilities required of the student in the workplace, e.g. how to wire a 13 amp plug, how to use a specific programme disc on a word-processor, how to operate the power take-off on a tractor, how specific safety devices on a machine work
- skills – practical abilities requiring more than just information and practice; such as how to make a dental patient feel more relaxed
- knowledge – the acquisition of relevant data and information *about* the subject area, i.e. what the student should know in a factual way
- understanding – the ability to translate passive knowledge into completing a task, e.g. to express data graphically, to appreciate and be able to discuss concepts and abstract ideas, to apply knowledge to the real world of action. This is the leap from 'knowing' into 'doing with reason and insight'.

19   *The practical aspects of learning, e.g. simulated work environments*
Many Further Education courses have a high level of practical learning built
into them, but only a portion of this happens in the work placement (see the
next heading). Much practical skill is acquired in college through simulated
work situations: the hair and beauty salons, the college farm, the market
garden, the plastering and electrical-installation bases, the teaching kitchen
and training restaurant. This section of the documentation should highlight
which competencies, skills, knowledge and understanding are to be taught and
learned. This section should indicate how a simulated environment will be set
up and used to bring about this learning.

20   *The work-placement requirements of the course*
Course documentation must set out the requirements of the programme for
attendance at work placement. It will give the kind of information which
students need to know, e.g.

- the timing, duration of attendance
- safety regulations
- what to do e.g. in the event of non-attendance through sickness
- the monitoring and assessment procedures.

It should also give the information needed by course planners, e.g.

- staff time allocations
- expectation about the nature and frequency of visits
- reporting requirements.

A list of placement locations is appropriate here, as well as the criteria used in
their selection.

21   *The teaching and learning methods to be promoted in the curriculum*
In Unit 5 we dealt with the traditional teaching skills. But we have already
emphasized in Unit 3 the need also to promote learning. This section of the
course documentation should articulate both. It should set out the ways in
which students can take initiatives and be responsible for their own learning – for example through the library, audio-visual or information-technology
services of the college, in home and private-study opportunities, by means of
classroom-based opportunities that have tutorial support and through opportunities for reflection on practice. Here, too, it is helpful to set out the aims of
teaching in the course; for example, that it is geared around questioning,
problem-solving and the encouragement of enquiry and independent thought.

22   *The assessment methods to be used for each component, practical and
theoretical*
Assessment should be part of the learning process, a facilitation of understanding rather than a hurdle to be jumped. Of course, it must also ensure standards,

both to the students and to the validators and potential employers. But assessment must not be something which comes as a surprise. Rather, the aims, nature and timing of assessments need to be articulated in detail, with timetables (where feasible) of when assessments will be set, when they should be handed in or completed and when the results will be known. The best assessment processes set down in advance the thinking behind the assessment task and the criteria against which performance is to be judged.

23   *The support, tutorial, profiling and reporting procedures of the course, including the commitment to equal opportunities*
Here it is reasonable to expect to find explained the ways in which both academic and personal support is to be offered to students. Much tutorial support, along with the assessment processes above, will be incorporated into the recording system. Unit 9 deals in more depth with recording. Unit 13 explores the issue of equal opportunities in greater detail.

24   *The success criteria or performance indicators for the course*
All courses must expect to be judged for efficiency and effectiveness. Here the course documentation should set down the *criteria* for such judgement, and usually these will be agreed with college boards and validators when a new course is established. Generally, the description 'performance indicators' is used of tangible and measurable criteria; typically, for example:

- the number of students who drop out and why
- the number who complete and qualify, and at what level
- the cost of the course per successful FTE student
- the number who go on to employment
- the number who go on to higher education, if applicable.

Success criteria can also include intangibles and those aspects which are less susceptible to measurement, for example:

- student satisfaction with the course
- good relations with the relevant industry
- effective teaching methods
- well-managed resources
- good course leadership.

25   *The processes for monitoring, reviewing and evaluating the course*
In the previous section, the course documentation was required to state success criteria. In this one, it should describe *how* the course is to be monitored, reviewed and evaluated. This will include the mechanisms used by course staff themselves to keep under scrutiny the progress of the course; the formal requirements of college quality-control mechanisms; and the periodic reviews

of validators. These processes must take account of not only staff perceptions, but those of students and of the appropriate employers and professional representatives.

Conclusion

The skill of thinking through and documenting courses is one which is absolutely crucial to all tutors in the present decade. For this reason we have emphasized the skills of the tutor in this aspect of his or her professional role.

In the Units which follow we take up and expand many of the themes which we have dealt with in outline here. If we have succeeded in our aim in the Unit, you will find the information contained in it a useful source of reference to which you will return when involved in course planning.

Unit 5

TEACHING SKILLS: QUESTIONING, EXPLAINING, SETTING TASKS

This Unit looks at some of the traditional skills of the tutor: the ability to explain clearly, to promote students' learning through questioning and to set meaningful and suitably demanding classroom tasks. While the whole of this book is about the skills required of the teacher in FE, it remains true that these three skills are the main weapons in every tutor's armoury. Just as a car driver cannot function effectively, however good his or her knowledge of the Highway Code, without the ability to steer, a knowledge of braking and an understanding of gears, so the tutor without practised and insightful explaining, questioning and task-setting abilities lacks direction and control over learning. The significance of these three skills cannot be over-emphasized; and even experienced practitioners can hone those skills even finer through reflection and self-analysis.

Giving clear explanations

Teachers in all kinds of classrooms, and with students of all ages, talk for much of the time; indeed, research suggests that an average teacher may talk for two-thirds of *all* lesson time. Increasingly, student-centred learning methods may be lessening that proportion, but it remains true that much teaching is still done through talk. Some of that talk would be classified as 'giving explanations'.

Explaining means giving understanding to another person. It involves an explainer (in our case, the tutor), explainees (students) and something to be explained (an aspect of the syllabus). Explaining functions through a set of linked statements, statements which are designed as the keys to unlock understanding.

Explanations can be of different kinds. *Interpretive* explanations are designed to answer 'What' questions in the minds of students: e.g., What is oil? Those explanations typically clarify terms, exemplify statements or throw light on issues. *Descriptive* explanations answer 'How' questions by describing processes, procedures or structures: e.g. 'How is oil produced?' Other explanations are *reason-giving*; that is, they anticipate 'Why' questions. These explanations involve reasons, motivations, justifications and causes: e.g. 'Why is oil an important fuel?'

Good explanations by the tutor do not just happen, they are the result of careful planning. To demonstrate how this works, carry out Task 13.

Task 13   Recalling and analysing an explanation you have just given

1   Think of an explanation you gave to a group of students recently or one you plan to give. Talk this explanation into a tape-recorder so that you can play it several times.

2   When you have completed this, but not before, look at the steps in planning an explanation set out in Table 5.

3   Compare your explanation with the steps in Table 5. How did your explanation, and the preparation for it, compare with the Table? Where did it differ?

4   How would you amend your explanation if you were to give it to another group?

TABLE 5   Steps in planning an explanation

- Analyse your topic into main parts or key areas.
- Establish the links between those key areas.
- Determine any rules involved.
- Specify the kind of explanation required (i.e. interpretive, descriptive, reason-giving).
- Adapt your planning to take account of the characteristics of the student group (more able, less able, etc.).

The language in which explanations are couched is especially important. Often an explanation will introduce technical terms or new concepts to the students; and these will need to be identified and themselves explained or defined early on. It is a mistake to appear too erudite by using wordy phrases or incomprehensible language: the language of good explanations will be explicit and direct and as simple as the subject allows. Similarly, the language of a good explanation will be precise, so that no confusion creeps in.

But language itself is not the only factor in delivering a good explanation. The way the explanation is delivered is important: the voice should be used to add emphasis where relevant, and the information can capture and control students' interest. Phraseology, too, can help to keep interest-levels high. As well as the voice itself, pauses and silence can give students moments to think, reflect and absorb. As the good explainer speaks, he or she will be sending out signals (sometimes these are called 'linguistic moves') – for example, words or phrases like 'first . . . ', 'next . . . ', 'then . . . ', 'an important point . . . '. A repetition or paraphrasing of key thoughts will serve the same purpose.

Finally, visual aids such as diagrams or working models may be introduced to reinforce the message which the words are conveying to the explainees.

Task 14   Examining your explanations for the linguistic factors of success

Play your sample explanation back. Does it have these hallmarks of good explaining:
- definitions of new and technical terms?
- clear and explicit language?
- precision of language, avoiding ambiguity?
- emphasis and interest in your voice?
- appropriate use of silence?
- 'linguistic moves' to help the student through the explanation?
- use of suitable visual materials?

You have now examined your own explaining technique twice, but Task 15 will ask you to do so once more. This time you will be looking for three more important skills in putting together good explanations.

First, the effective explainer will use examples to illustrate the points he or she is trying to make. These examples will be clear, appropriate and concrete. There will be enough of them to carry the explainees along; and they will be both positive and negative, i.e. they will show how the matter in question does operate and how it does not.

Second, the effective explanation will show evidence of being organized. It will have a clear and logical sequence, and it will be held together by the use of link phrases. Its argument will move the listener on in a step-by-step progressive sequence.

Third, the explainer will insert into the explanation opportunities for questions, and will pause to assess whether the audience is in fact following the explanation, learning from it and weighing its implications.

Task 15   Looking for some key skills in your own explanations

Go back over your recorded explanation again. Seek in it evidence of the factors described above:
- use of examples
- organization
- feedback.

When you have completed Task 15 in this Unit, you will have overhauled your explaining technique against important and rigorous criteria. You should try to ensure that these criteria become part of your continuing approach to explaining. Finally in this section, Table 6 points up some common errors in explaining and explanations.

TABLE 6   Common errors in explaining and explanations

- The explainer fails to understand the topic him/herself.
- The explainer misses out a link or 'key'.
- The explanation is rushed.
- The language of the explanation is not understood by all.
- The explainer forgets that instructions (as well as curriculum content) may need explanation.
- The feedback or evaluation stages are omitted.

Asking effective questions

Many of the verbal transactions in classrooms are tutor talk of the kind described above. But tutors also ask questions – a lot of questions. It has been calculated that the average teacher in a secondary school may ask 1.5 million questions in a professional lifetime; some will ask twice this number. There is no reason to believe that FE tutors ask substantially less questions than other teachers. Clearly, a process which consumes so much tutor-energy should be honed to an efficient level. So questioning, like explaining, is a major area for skill development of which all tutors should be aware. Table 7 suggests some reasons for using questions as a means to student learning.

TABLE 7 Reasons for using questions in the classroom

Some possible reasons are:

- to encourage students to talk constructively and on-task
- to signal an interest in hearing what students feel and think
- to stimulate interest and awaken curiosity
- to encourage a problem-solving approach to thinking and learning
- to help students externalize and verbalize knowledge
- to encourage 'thinking aloud' and exploratory approaches to tasks – the 'intuitive leap'
- to help students to learn from each other and to respect and evaluate each other's contributions
- to monitor the students' learning, its extent, level and deficiencies
- to deepen students' thinking levels and improve their ability to conceptualize.

This section asks you to take a detached and objective look at the questions which you ask, and to try to analyse their effectiveness.

▶ Task 16   Exploring your own questioning technique

To carry out the analyses in this section you will need some examples of questions you have asked. *Before you read on*, set aside some time when you are likely to be engaged in a teaching session which will involve you asking questions – preferably a session forty–sixty minutes long. Tape-record the session.

When you have completed Task 16 you will have a reasonable sample of your own questions available for close scrutiny. Armed with this sample, you can begin to look at different aspects of questioning skill.

Most questions can be classified into two kinds: closed questions and open questions.

Closed questions require a single word or very brief response, for which there is a single correct answer and the answer has been predetermined by the questioner, e.g. 'What is the chemical formula for iron oxide?'

Open questions require an answer running to a sentence or more, where a variety of responses could be acceptable to the questions and where there may be no 'correct answer', e.g. 'How would you assess the character of Henry VIII?'

Task 17 Assessing your use of open questions

Go back over your tape-recorded lesson and record for each question you asked whether it was closed or open.

If the result of Task 17 is the discovery that most of your questions were closed, then your style of questioning could be regarded as exhibiting the characteristics on the left of the continua below. If most of the questions proved to be open, then your style probably veers to the right.

Didactic style ———————	Informal style
Based on tutor-centred instruction ———————	Based on student-centred learning
Directed to pre-determined answers———————	Directed to a range of acceptable responses
Arising from content-orientated teaching ———————	Arising from process-orientated teaching

Your style of questioning might give away quite a lot about your approaches to teaching/learning. But the type of questions you ask may also indicate the kinds and levels of cognitive demands you make on students. The next task asks you to analyse your questions in terms of these cognitive demands by using the analysis system in Table 8.

Task 18   Analysing the cognitive demands of questions

1   Study the analysis system in Table 8 until you have mastered it.
2   Replay your recorded lesson.
3   Analyse each question according to the types listed in Table 8.
4   Complete the box below.

No. of questions in:					
Type 1	Type 2	Type 3	Type 4	Type 5	Type 6
=	=	=	=	=	=

Total Type 1 + 2	Total type 3 + 4 + 5 + 6
= (i.e. lower-order)	= (i.e. higher-order)

% lower-order = % higher-order = $\dfrac{}{100\%}$

5   Using the measures from Tasks 16 and 17, how do you rate your skill as a questioner? What do you do well, and what could be improved?

TABLE 8   Question types and levels of cognitive demand

1   RECALL QUESTIONS ask students to remember information they have previously learned; e.g. 'What instrument did we use to make this measurement?'

2   SIMPLE COMPREHENSION QUESTIONS ask students to repeat information already supplied by the tutor in the lesson: 'Why did we say we needed to . . . ?'

Lower-order questions (above) ask students to reproduce knowledge. Higher-order questions (below) ask students to *use* knowledge.

3   APPLICATION QUESTIONS ask the students to understand a general principle and apply it in new situations; e.g. 'What theorem would you use to find the size of this angle?' 'How would you deal with this client's complaint?'

4   ANALYSIS QUESTIONS ask the students to break down subject-matter into its parts, and to study the nature of those parts and of the relationship between them; e.g. 'Why does Graham Greene choose to start the novel in that unusual way?' 'Why would you use treatment x rather than treatment y on this client?'

5   SYNTHESIS QUESTIONS ask the students to build a new idea, plan or experiment; e.g. 'How would the view of the world put across in this play affect your attitude towards friendship and trust?'

6   EVALUATION QUESTIONS ask students to make judgements particularly about quality; e.g. 'To what extent are we convinced by the justice of the cause in this article, and how far are we swayed by good writing?' 'Why do you prefer this design to that one?'

Tutors spend, typically, a good deal of time and many questions in the reinforcement of knowledge through lower-order questions and relatively less in promoting thinking through higher-order questions with an enhanced level of cognitive demand. It is *not* possible, or desirable, that all questions should be pitched at the higher levels; the aim of this analysis is rather

- to alert tutors to the learning potential of asking higher-order questions, and
- through that awareness, to encourage an increase in the freqeuncy and a more self-conscious use of higher-order questions to promote learning.

Interestingly, when research was carried out into the use of higher-order questions in school classrooms it was discovered that primary-school pupils were asked a greater proportion of higher-order questions than secondary pupils were. One factor in the explanation for this was undoubtedly that the secondary schools were more content-laden and syllabus-bound. This is a danger inherent in many FE courses, too. Table 9 summarizes some of the skills that tutors need and common mistakes that tutors make when using questions.

TABLE 9   Basic questioning skills and some things to avoid

Basic skills

- Preparing teaching sessions around key questions
- Making sure the language/content level is appropriate to the students
- If students cannot answer, prompting and giving clues
- Distributing questions evenly around the group
- Using student responses – even the wrong ones
- Pausing long enough to allow thinking-time
- Making progressive cognitive demands

Things to avoid

- Repeating one's questions
- Repeating students' questions
- Answering one's own questions
- Questioning for chorus answering

The tutor's role in the classroom has traditionally been seen as one of chalk-and-talk. Throughout this book, clearly, we have implied that tutors have a much broader and more professionally demanding role than this. Nevertheless, talk – explanations and questions – is indeed the epitome of the tutor's skill; and the two foregoing sections of this Unit have suggested how performance can be improved and refined in this area. The next step is to apply similar principles to that other 'stock-in-trade' of the tutor: setting work to students. We prefer to think of the resulting activities as classroom tasks.

Setting classroom tasks

Tutors set tasks to students on a regular basis. Sometimes the tasks are for completion there and then, sometimes in private-study periods, sometimes at home. Some tasks will be of a practical nature (construct a model, carry out a survey); some will be of a more traditional 'academic' nature (work out through examples in maths or modern languages, write an essay). Some will be examination or assessment orientated; others will simply be to reinforce or extend students' classroom or placement work. All of these activities, whether brief or extended in nature, are classroom tasks.

Task-setting behaviour by tutors can vary considerably and, as with driving a car, it is possible to develop bad habits or simply to forget to be self-critical. This section is aimed at making tutors more self-aware of their task-setting behaviour. As in other sections of this Unit, you are asked in the next Task to carry out some monitoring of your own practice.

Task 19   Monitoring your own task-setting

1   Select a period of two or three weeks in the middle of a term when you will be seeing a regular series of classes.
2   Record every task you set throughout this period. Make a list like the one below:

Nature of task	Purpose of task	Target student group
1		
2		
3		

3   When you have completed your survey, move onto the rest of this section.

One factor in effective task-setting is to sustain interest and variety for students. Of course, tutors are constrained *in part* by the requirements of examination boards or of assessment procedures; but in reality, tutors set many more tasks to students than are bound by these narrow constraints. In Task 20 you are asked to examine the interest-level of the tasks you set.

Task 20   Putting interest and variety into task-setting

1   Look back over the tasks you set to students over your chosen two–three week period. Try to categorize the tasks you set. The following headings may help you to do this; add your own as required.
   ● written essays
   ● working through formal exercises
   ● problem-solving
   ● reading (with/without note-taking)
   ● making drawings, models, plans, displays, etc.
   ● preparing materials for work experience
   ● writing up e.g. work diaries, experiments.

2   Now decide precisely how varied a diet of tasks your students experience. Could this be improved? How? Formulate a strategy for more varied task-setting in your classes.

Earlier in this Unit, in the section on questioning, it was suggested that questions can be pitched at various levels to elicit different levels of cognitive performance from students. In many ways, classroom tasks are simply another kind of questioning – more elaborate, more formalized, often requiring a response in writing or in action rather than through the spoken word, but questioning nevertheless. Just as questions can be pitched at various levels of cognitive demand, so can these tasks. Table 10 sets out a way of analysing tasks by cognitive demand.

TABLE 10   Analysing tasks through cognitive demand

Type	Example(s) or definition
Reinforcing tasks (low)	Writing up work covered in class; note-taking from texts; working on examples (in maths, modern languages) of known material.
Imaginative tasks (high)	Using the skills of creativity, empathy, sympathy to complete work.
Problem-solving or reasoning tasks (high)	Using skills of data collection to solve a problem, hypothesize, deduce or work out answers where not all the information is provided.
Application tasks (high)	Using knowledge or information in an applied setting, e.g. given specific symptoms, what first aid would be required on a particular casualty?

| Analytical tasks (high) | These ask the question: Why? Analytical tasks ask students to differentiate between facts and hypotheses, to find patterns, clarify relationships, etc. |
| Evaluative tasks (high) | Such tasks ask students to appraise, assess or criticize according to justified criteria. E.g. 'How objective is this piece of news reporting?' Or 'What are the arguments for and against a barrage in the Severn Estuary?' |

Task 21   Analysing your sample tasks for cognitive demand

1   Go back over your sample of tasks set to students. Categorize each task, using Table 10 as a guide. Adapt the categories or add new ones if required, but make sure your new categories measure cognitive demand.

2   What proportion of your tasks fell to lower and what to higher cognitive levels of demand?

3   Could you have made more cognitive demand on students? Would the resulting tasks have been more interesting as a result?

4   Do your marking and assessment systems take account of the cognitive demand of tasks, with more weight given to higher-order tasks and less weight to lower-order ones?

5   Given the results of Tasks 19 and 20, what would you do to improve your approach to task-setting?

Finally in this section it would repay you to give some thought to a range of other issues about task-setting which may help you to shape your classroom performance:

• Are the tasks you set differentiated, i.e. do you set one task to the whole group, or do you (regularly, when appropriate) set different tasks to different individuals/groups according to need?

• Do you build in a variety of ways in which, over time, students can respond to tasks? E.g. do they always write responses, or can they use media such as tape, photographs, etc.?

• If you teach several classes similar work, do you set different tasks, or the same, to each class?

• When you set tasks, do you explain to the students in language they can appreciate what the aims of the task are in cognitive terms?

Remember task-setting is not about keeping students in check by having to jump unforeseen hurdles; it is about helping to facilitate their journey on the road to understanding and insight.

Conclusion

This Unit has concentrated on some very fundamental teaching skills, skills required of all tutors in every kind of student group and in every curriculum area. In particular, it has been stressed that a fundamental ability of the tutor is to get students to think more analytically, rigorously and effectively. This Unit stands at the heart of everything that is said in this book; but there are several especially strong links with other Units, and it may be worthwhile to draw attention to these. First, the Unit implies that the students' thinking and contributions should be valued, a theme picked up from Unit 1 on relationships. Second, this Unit has looked at task-setting as a skill, but there are links ahead to Unit 9 on recording and profiling, to Unit 7 on responding to students' written work, and to Unit 11 on adult students. Finally, but not exhaustively, this Unit concentrates on specific teaching skills, from which Unit 6 continues with the generic skills of managing learning.

Unit 6

TEACHING SKILLS: THE ORGANIZATION AND MANAGEMENT OF LEARNING

In the previous Unit we looked at some traditional teaching skills: significant weapons in the armoury of the teacher. In this Unit we shift our attention to how learning and teaching are organized and managed, and at some of the things that tutors can do to refine these aspects of their performance. The first requirement of organization and management in the classroom is preparation.

Preparing lessons and preparing for lessons

The skill of effective preparation is essential to all teachers in all phases of education – preparation needs to be done at two levels:

- preparing the lesson
- preparing for the lesson.

The first of these relates to the need to prepare lesson material and plan out how it is to be delivered. There are some key steps in this. These, typically, include:

- identifying the intentions of the lesson
- setting down the knowledge, understanding, skills and competencies which students will acquire from it

- doing any necessary background study at your own level
- sequencing the material to be taught
- identifying a 'snappy' beginning
- fitting the work into the overall syllabus
- deciding on its relation to assessment activities
- identifying teaching methods (see Unit 5)
- preparing differentiated tasks for different students (see Unit 5)
- identifying teaching modes (whole class, group work, self-study)
- collecting resources
- deciding on accommodation needs
- preparing specific hand-outs, etc.
- deciding on an interesting lesson-ending
- keeping your own records of work covered.

Preparing for the lesson includes the organizational activities which the tutor may have to carry out to make the well-planned lesson run smoothly on the day. Below is a list of just some of the organization tasks a tutor may have to do to prepare for lessons:

- organize a classroom display to support the topic
- book a specific room or location, e.g. a lecture theatre, laboratory
- hire or borrow a video
- book audio-visual equipment
- get hand-outs run off through a centralized printing system
- book a speaker (see Unit 16)
- prepare a resource collection in the classroom to support self-study
- adjust the layout of the accommodation
- have paper, texts, materials, etc., ready.

Task 22   Preparing lessons

Have an honest look at all the lessons you have delivered in the last week. Use the two checklists above to discover how effective your preparation was. Identify any omissions. Resolve how to put these right in future.

In the sections of this Unit which follow, we pick up some of these themes again in more detail, as well as adding some new dimensions.

Keeping variety in lessons

Tutors may develop their skills to quite a high degree, but if they are not used in a *variety* of ways, then the teaching/learning taking place can become unstimulating and stagnant!

The key is 'variety': variety in teaching methods and variety in learning experiences/situations. In addressing this, you need to look first at the aims of your course. You should ask yourself how the teaching and learning strategies you employ will encourage this fulfilment of your intentions and objectives. You need to think, too, about how to involve your students more in their own learning, address work-based or work-related problems, and how to use the real-life experiences they gain whilst on work placement.

Task 23   Seeking variety in lessons

Look back over lessons you have taught in the last four weeks. Using the list below, note down how and when each of the types of teaching and learning strategies were employed by you and your students.

- Variety in modes of assignment:
    - experimental
    - interpretive
    - time-constrained
    - observational
    - practical (role play)
- Student-centred learning – in which the student is free to develop his or her own line of thinking on self-chosen topic of interest
- Use of experiential learning from placement and other sources
- Integrated assignments – where two or more units of the course combined to show linkage, understanding and application
- Assessment strategies:
    - tutor assessment
    - self-assessment
    - peer-group assessment
    - assessment by placing supervisors
    - external assessment – moderators/examiners
- Assessment of common or transferable skills (using some or all of the above strategies)

Finally, rate yourself overall for variety of approach.

Core themes and common or transferable skills

In Unit 1 we emphasized the need for all tutors involved with a particular course to give consistent messages about teaching and learning skills.

Your teaching skills need to be developed in terms of co-ordinating the students' learning in that they receive the same 'messages' from all course team members. This can be done by working on the development of the same common skills in *all units* of the course. The same core themes can also punctuate your course content, to establish a standard 'package' for all students. Each and every individual is different and will respond to learning experiences in a different way; but provision must be carefully planned by all tutors and never appear to be uncoordinated or contradictory.

Table 11 sets out some common or transferable skills which might be central to any course.

TABLE 11   Some common themes and transferable skills

- Self-development
- Learning and studying skills
- Self-management and organization
- Time management
- Working with others
- Communication skills
- Information-seeking
- Using information technology
- Skills of analysis and using evidence
- Numeracy skills
- Skills of data display
- Identifying and tackling problems
- Practical skills
- Understanding the role of science technology
- Design skills
- Understanding environmental issues
- Health and safety-consciousness
- Equal-opportunity awareness
- Appreciating gender issues
- Developing 'people skills'.

Task 24 Exploring the use of transferable skills

1   Look at the list of transferable skills in Table 11.
2   Now examine your own course to see:
   - which of these themes are covered
   - which of these are omitted (and why)
   - which of these should be added
   - which additional skills your course includes or should include
3   Talk to your fellow tutors about your findings.

Using resources and materials effectively

Good preparation is a vital teaching skill which involves the use of materials and equipment. A feature of Further Education colleges in the 1990s is lack of finance for resources; therefore the existing equipment needs to be utilized carefully and intensively by staff.

In setting up a new course or revamping an existing one, it is a good idea to assess available resources and plan their use carefully. This is sometimes a difficult task – buildings can make transportation and use of equipment arduous! You may require an overhead projector for a lesson, but you could find yourself having to carry it up a flight of stairs if there aren't any available on your floor. Use of a video can pose problems too; if you need to book into a particular room, e.g. an audio-visual room/specialist classroom weeks in advance because of high demand. Specialist help too, in the form of support staff, is sometimes difficult to obtain because of low resourcing, e.g. if problems occur in transportation or use of equipment. Therefore, you need to find out how much help is available and where to find assistance. Above all, if possible, book help in advance: so be aware of booking procedures.

It is a good idea to draw up a list of all your course units and subject areas, and devise a plan of resources (just as you did for staff resources in Unit 4) as in Table 12. (In Table 12 we have used numbers to indicate sections of a hypothetical course.)

TABLE 12   Analysing resource needs: an example

Course units or subject areas	Specialist accommodation	Equipment
3, 2, 5, 7, 9, 12	Base-room	Overhead projector, video (shares with three other rooms). Student lockers, camcorder (shared with all rooms on same floor), 3 cameras.
4, 8	Computer room	10 BBC microcomputers, 10 Apple-macs, 4 Amstrads, 2 Archimedes, printers, software.
1, 6	Health room	First aid facilities, overhead projector, home nursing equipment, Resusci-Annie, Resusci-baby.
10	Home economics room	Gas and electric cookers, microwave ovens, washer, tumble dryer, dishwasher and cooking equipment.
11, 12	Biology laboratory	Overhead projector, 2 computers with software relevant for environmental science, health and biology. 15 microscopes and anatomical models.

Task 25   Analysing your classroom resource needs

Following the format in Table 12, list all the resources necessary for your subject areas. Make a separate note of all the equipment you would like to obtain if and when the funds are made available.

Library resources

A very important part of teaching and learning is the use of the *library facility*. Students need to be made aware of the opportunities for learning and studying available in the college library; these will often include:

- large selection of books for loan/reference
- study booths and study tables
- photocopier
- librarian and library assistants
- microfiche system
- card catalogue
- computers
- videos
- large selection of periodicals.

The students need to be shown how to make best use of these facilities; e.g. their attention can be drawn to key periodicals which can act as excellent reinforcers. This process can be an integral part of student induction.

Access

The question students will ask about resources is how and when they can use them. They need to know access times for the library facility and when they can have access to computers, overhead projectors, camcorders, video equipment, etc. It is therefore necessary to find out and pass on all the college rules and regulations for student use of equipment.

Being vigilant

Earlier in this Unit it was suggested that preparation of and for lessons was a key to good classroom management and organization. This remains true. But good organization does not stop there: what happens in the classroom is, obviously, important too. However well prepared one is, however well organized the learning environment is and however well resources are deployed, the final interactions are the human ones between tutor and students. In Unit 1 we discussed the broad issues of relationships which underlie effective teaching. Here, we are going on to look at two aspects of tutor behaviour which can affect both relationships and learning. The first is the skill of vigilance.

An effective class manager both knows what is going on in the classroom, and controls the activity. Both of these functions require us to develop the skill of vigilance. In practice, while we may not walk around with our proverbial eyes shut, most of us definitely need to sharpen up on our ability not just to see, but to see with insight, what is happening in the busy environment of our classrooms. Since the visual signals we receive amount to hundreds an hour, and always several simultaneously, it is no easy skill.

The next Task, 26, asks you to try to pair up with a fellow tutor as critical friend. You can even swap roles later! This takes some courage but the lessons learned will be worth the misgivings.

 ## Task 26   Observing the skill of vigilance

1   Look at the observation schedule in Table 13
2   Ask a colleague to watch one of your lessons, recording the data required in the Table.

TABLE 13   An observation schedule for examining a tutor's skills of vigilance

Date ....

Class ....

Subject ....

(To the observer: make brief notes about the lesson in the spaces below. Look through the whole schedule so that you know what must be done during the lesson.)

1 EYES   For approximately the first ten minutes of the lesson watch the tutor's eyes. Does he/she look at the class when explaining or questioning? When students are working alone or in groups does the teacher look around the room or only at the nearest group? Make notes on the tutor's use of eye contact and vigilance.

2 INDIVIDUAL   Choose two students who do not appear to be applying themselves to
   STUDENTS   their task. Study these two carefully and make notes about their behaviour. What do they do? What contacts do they have with the tutor? Do they solicit these or does the tutor? Is there any indication from what you see or hear as to why they are not involved in their work?

                         Student A: Name ....(if known; if not, brief desciption)

Student B: Name   .... (if known;
if not, brief description)

3   Together, analyse the results.
4   Swap roles.

The exercise in Task 26 should have alerted you to your ability to *observe* what is happening in your classroom. Since more and more teaching in the Further Education sector involves the use of group work, usually alongside students working individually, we should not leave the topic of classroom management without casting a glance at the tutor in this less didactic and more facilitating interactive role.

The tutor's role as facilitator

The tutor's role while groups of students are involved in working together (and semi-independently) is varied. It is of course different from the major role of instructor during class teaching. The ability to perform successfully the skills involved in these other roles must contribute in large measure to the success of group work. For example, a tutor who is not able to see that equipment and resources are provided, or whose organizing powers are limited, will probably find the organization and implementation of group work beyond him or her.

The tutor who finds it difficult to move from the front, and to interact at a more personal level with individuals, will probably not be inclined to tackle group work.

Group work, then, involves skills different from, and over and above, those used in class teaching. Within the lesson students must be kept working separately from the teacher and must not be allowed to drift. The tutor has to keep tabs on activities minute by minute. At the same time he or she is involved in individual and group tuition; explaining and questioning. He/she has to motivate the students, keep track of everyone's progress, and control and supervise, as well as keep his/her own sanity. Outside the lesson there is research and preparation, possibly with attendant problems of the storage and retrieval of resource material.

Task 27 aims to list and analyse activities in which the tutor engages during a group lesson.

Task 27   Examining the tutor's role as facilitator

1   Choose one of your own classes and ask a fellow tutor to sit in on the lesson. (Alternatively, observe a lesson with group teaching given by an experienced colleague.) In the lesson use the grid given in Table 14.
2   Carry out the following activities after the observed lesson:
   • Observer and tutor should compare notes about, and impressions of, the lesson.
   • Write a brief note on the teaching skills and roles which are particularly involved in group work.
   • Compare your findings with those from research at Nottingham University. In group work, the teacher was found to act as consultant and facilitator more than as instructor and questioner. These latter two roles ranked as highly as those of organizer and provider of equipment. A teacher rarely acted as a disciplinary agent.

consultant
facilitator   frequent roles

instructor
questioner
organizer   less frequent
provider

disciplinarian   rare

TABLE 14   Observation proforma for observing the tutor's role in group work lessons

The observer fills in sections 1, 2 and 3 during the lesson.

SECTION 1   THE ROLE OF THE TUTOR
Tick as appropriate

| | | FREQUENCY | |
What roles did the tutor play during group work?	Used frequently	Used once or twice	Not used
Motivator			
Facilitator			
Consultant			
Disciplinary agent			
Instructor			
Questioner			
Setter of social climate			
Organizer			
Provider of equipment and other resources			
Other (specify)			
Add your own comments			

SECTION 2   MOVING AROUND

Plot the groups on a classroom plan below. For ten minutes track the tutor's movements between groups. Indicate how long is spent with each group. Try also to note the vigilance extended to other groups while any one group is being attended to.

(Draw your classroom plan here)

SECTION 3   CONTACT
For ten minutes note the frequency of contacts between tutor and students, both tutor-initiated and student-initiated ones:

Tutor-initiated contact:

Student-initiated contact:

How long, or for what percentage of the task in hand, can a group work without teacher contact?

If you are teaching this lesson, complete section 4.
SECTION 4   MOBILITY AND VIGILANCE
Straight after the lesson fill in this section yourself.
Mobility   Were you sufficiently mobile between groups so that students' work was able to proceed smoothly or was there, for example, 'dead time' while a group waited for you?

Vigilance   Were you deaf and blind to all groups except the one you were with?

Informing and managing

From the previous sections of this Unit it will, hopefully, have become clear that successful classroom management is affected by the tutor's behaviour outside the classroom (e.g. in preparation) and inside it (e.g. through skills such as vigilance and facilitation). At this point it is worthwhile reminding the reader that Unit 1, on handling relations with students, is a useful cross-reference; and that Unit 3, too, has important messages related to effective management of the learning process. Finally, in this Unit, it is opportune to point out the important relationship between managing and sustaining the flow of information.

Efficient course management will require all tutors to pass on good quality information about the course, and to do so in good time. In Unit 4 we looked at designing and documenting curriculum, and we assumed that curriculum documentation would be available to students. To put it colloquially but succinctly, we suggested there that students need to know 'where they are' in terms of the respect and trust we generate, and 'where they are up to' in terms of syllabus, course work, assessment and examinations.

It is worth belabouring here the need to pass information in a continuous but relevant flow. The disciplined use of a noticeboard should be encouraged. Here are just some of the things that might appear on it:

- course structure
- course timetable
- placement dates
- assignment details and deadlines
- exam dates
- forthcoming events, e.g. speakers, meetings, items required for particular sessions
- tutorial timetable.

Being informed and managing

Finally, in this Unit, we turn the tables and look at what students can tell us as tutors to inform our organization and management.

If students are to be seen as truly important then their views on the teaching and learning they experience are essential data for tutors. We would strongly recommend, therefore, regular consultation with students about *their* perceptions of the learning on offer.

It is possible at the end of the academic year to provide students with a questionnaire which will assess both teaching and learning strategies employed. Students should also be given the opportunity to provide constructively analytical comments on various aspects of the course management and organization. The following is not intended to be a usable questionnaire for all courses, but a basic 'idea bank' on which you can draw to make up your own questionnaire. You might seek opinions about:

- teaching methods
- preferred learning methods
- assessment activities
- work placement
- course information
- visual aids
- videos
- demonstrations
- guest speakers
- practical lessons
- role-playing exercises
- case-studies
- visits
- lectures
- discussions
- individual work
- group work
- recommended books
- handouts
- facilities, e.g. library provision.

Here are some useful prompting questions:

- Was the unit difficult?
- Was it interesting?
- Was it valuable?
- Were you satisfied with it?
- Were the aims clear?
- Did you fully understand it?
- Was there enough time available?

So here is a final point:

Tutors and students are the major stakeholders in the educative process. If one becomes disorganized and the other disenchanted, both perish.

Unit 7

SETTING AND RESPONDING TO STUDENTS' WRITTEN WORK

The purpose and audiences for written work

We have included a self-contained Unit on this theme because we believe that there are aspects of these teaching/learning skills which are essential to the FE teacher and that they are skills to which too little attention is paid. Think back to your own education. Certainly before the age of 16 and probably after that, written work may well have consisted in the main of essays, and marking probably meant the teacher covering large areas of them with what might be caricatured as 'red ink and corrections'. This kind of response to students' work still lingers on but is, we suggest, inappropriate. A good starting point for looking at students' written work is to examine two related questions about it:

- What is the purpose of the work?
- Who, therefore, will be the audience for it?

In Table 15 there are two columns. On the left are some examples of the kind of work which you might, from time to time, ask students to undertake. On the right are some suggested audiences for that written work.

TABLE 15   Types of students' written work and their main audiences

Type of work	Main audience(s)
Course-work essays	Tutor – to track progress Student – for revision
Lecture notes and recording of other classroom activities, e.g. write-ups of experiments, practical work done in class	Student – for later study and reference
Extended studies, project work	Tutor – as internal assessor Student – for later reference
Placement preparation material	Tutor – to check preparation Student – for reference
Work-placement diaries or continuous records	Tutor Placement supervisor – for assessment External moderator Student – for later reference
Précis material from texts	Student – for acquisition and revision of knowledge
Answers to mock exam questions	Tutor – for monitoring Student – to indicate progress
Revision tests	Tutor – possibly for monitoring Student – for self-checking
Worked examples	Student – for practice

Task 28   Examining types of students' written work and their intended audiences

Look at Table 15 and examine the two columns in it. Decide whether the lists are exhaustive for the kinds of work you set. Add, or delete, any categories in each column which do not fit your particular circumstances.

Table 15 and Task 28 probably bring home the point quite forcibly that the *consistent* audience for all written work is the student him/herself. The student is at the heart of the process. But, even more importantly, *the student needs to understand this*. A good piece of work is like an investment: it has value now and may produce more rewards in the future, not necessarily in terms of marks but because it can be a reference point. A bad piece of work sells only one person short – its creator! Students often talk about doing good or bad written work *for* Miss X or Mr Y; but really they always do it fundamentally *for themselves*. Once this point has been established with a class it is possible to move on to other equally important issues about written work.

Identifying purposes and criteria for written work in advance

How often have we, as students, experienced or witnessed tutors who have set written tasks like this:

'Today I'm going to get you to write an account of the ground we covered last lesson.'

'For homework I want you to do the first six questions on page 104.'

'This session we are going to practise an exam question. Here it is, on the sheet I'm giving out: you have 45 minutes starting now.'

This pattern of operation is often, we believe, not just ineffective but fails to maximize the potential learning which students could get from the task. What is needed to make these, and similar, tasks meaningful is a prior identification by the tutor of the purposes of the task, the communication of those purposes to the students, and the spelling out *in advance* of the criteria by which success in the task will be judged. Perhaps the best way to illustrate this is through an example. Table 16 provides an example and may be useful as a model from which you can develop your own technique.

▶ ## Task 29   Identifying purposes and criteria for written tasks

Study the information in Table 16, and then consider these questions.
I   Look back over written tasks you have set to students in the last month. Analyse them according to the proforma in Table 16:
- Have you always identified the audiences for the tasks you have set?
- Have you always set out the purposes of the task?

TABLE 16   A possible model for task-setting in the FE class

Target group: Twenty 16-plus students on a general education course

Background: The students will enter a GCSE exam which involves a study of environmental science. One section of the syllabus requires them to have a knowledge of factors which pollute the environment. Part of the exam may involve writing an essay on the pollution theme. They have reached the stage of studying written sources and videos and had class discussions about rival methods of producing electrical energy. The tutor decides it would be a useful moment to crystallize what has been learned and do so through a response to an essay question. She therefore supplies the following set of instructions about the task, as a handout, to each class member.

The task

1   In this task you are going to be asked to tackle the sort of question you might be set in your exam paper.

2   In the exam you would have about forty minutes to answer the question, BUT it will be useful to you to do a more thorough answer which you can use for revision later.

3   So I am going to ask you to do this essay not as a practice question but in private-study time, and to spend about 1½ hours doing it in some detail.

4   Please hand the work in in ten days' time: that is, *on 7 May*.

5   The following set out the things I, or an examiner, would expect to find in the answer – so these are the things you will be assessed on.

Criteria

(a)   Is the essay properly structured, readable and in reasonable English, with a clear beginning and end?

(b)   Can you accurately describe the process of producing electricity, from both nuclear sources and from coal?

(c)   Do you know, and can you list, the advantages and disadvantages for both systems?

(d)   Can you use your knowledge to reach a sensible conclusion and argue for it, as the question requires?

●   Have you laid out *in advance* the criteria against which the tasks will be judged?

2   Consider your answers in (1). What do these tell you about your own task-setting?

3   How can you now go on to improve your task-setting strategies? (Don't just follow the ideas given in this chapter; be rigorous in adapting to your own curriculum area and the needs of your students.)
4   Try asking the students what would help them to respond better to written tasks.
5   Would fewer, but more effective, written tasks help the workload of both you and your students?

Marking written work

What has been said in this chapter clearly indicates quite strong views about the purposes of setting written tasks and about the nature of written tasks as carefully designed learning experiences. It would not be possible to give hard-and-fast guidelines about grading systems because these will differ with, for example

- curriculum area
- context and type of task
- college or departmental policy.

What is clear is that *one* aspect of marking is to know what the grading system is, and to communicate it and its significance to the students. Grading must ultimately be seen as feedback to students about task performance: just as they were central to the process of task-setting, so they must be central to the systems that are used to value the work done.

Task 30   Examining your grading and assessment systems for written work

1   Look over the grading and assessment systems that are used to judge written work by students on the courses you teach.
2   Make a list (in each case) of what you perceive to be their strengths and weaknesses. How do you think they could be improved?
3   How do your views in (2) match with student views?

But if one aspect of marking is the use made of a grading system and the effectiveness of the resulting feedback, another must be the *literal* marking of the work – the marks you make on the student's pages and the overt and covert messages you convey by them. Let's look at extreme cases.

Example 1 The student's essay is covered in red ink, with dozens of small errors of punctuation, grammar and spelling corrected in large letters. One paragraph is scratched through. There are several places where the tutor has written 'No!' 'DO YOU REALLY THINK THIS?' and so on in the margins or at the end of the paragraph. The grade on the bottom is recorded as 5½/10. There is no summary comment at the end.

Example 2 The student's essay is largely free of corrections of minor errors of English, though some repeated misspellings of key words are listed at the end. Much of the text is otherwise unmarked by the tutor's pencil. At the bottom of the last page is the following comment:

'The first paragraph on page 3 is factually incorrect – look at your textbook page 169 and the diagram on page 170. The remainder of the essay shows you understand most of the information about this topic; but you haven't thought out e.g. *why* the sales manager took this action or *what else* he could have done. Jot some notes about these two issues on the back of this page so it will help you revise. Because it's mostly sound on facts this would probably pass – but to get a good mark you need to deal with *reasons* and *issues*.'

Task 31 Responding to examples of marking

1   Look at the two examples of marking just given. As a *tutor* , which do you prefer and why?
2   Imagine you are a student: which would you prefer, and why?
3   Now it can be revealed that they are two tutors' responses to the *same* piece of work by a student. What does that tell you about the markers?
4   What lessons have you learned from this Task which you could apply to your own situation?

Reflections on setting and responding to written work

We all of us feel vulnerable when we are judged; so as professionals we need to make proper vigorous assessments while retaining sensitivity to the effect these have on our students. The messages of this Unit have been simple ones, but perhaps especially significant because of their very simplicity. Yet it remains true that some readers might ask why it is necessary to spell out such simple messages. The reasons are, perhaps, more tortuous than the messages.

Think back to your own school days and to exams you took, particularly in the Arts. Sometimes you, or others, wrote excellent pieces of work but you had to work hard to get above 70 per cent; and full marks were deemed impossible. Nor did anyone really explain what the missing 30 per cent really represented: it was a kind of pedagogic black hole!

In the same way – albeit rarely – one comes across a tutor who tries to prevent students' access to past papers from examinations, and even to syllabus documents! Obviously such acts are unreasonable or worse; but they represent an insecurity about 'letting the students in on the learning process', perhaps, lest they make judgements about the teaching process.

What is advocated here is the fullest possible articulation to students, and between tutors and students, about the process of learning and the criteria for assessing improvement or success in written performance.

In Units 5, 6 and 7 we have looked very directly at the teaching and learning processes inside classrooms. In Unit 8 we step outside the classroom into the work placement.

Unit 8

HANDLING PLACEMENT IN WORK EFFECTIVELY

The aims of work placement

. . . It's another hectic day in the workplace. Staff are absent. You are trying to do ten jobs at once. The phone rings:

> 'This is Mrs Evans from Smithedon College. How are you fixed for taking on a Work Experience placement next month, starting 22nd?'

You sit in stunned silence trying to work out how you will cope with the end-of-year accounts, get out all those important reports that the Boss wants urgently. Will the staff be back by then?

> 'Yes, great. No problem at all.'

This was the reaction of one workplace supervisor of students from a Further Education course. In an office, a factory, a hospital, school or hairdressing salon, the story is the same. Busy people, with heavy workloads, yet many of them are willing to spend time organizing the work experience. The few who consider the student to be 'an extra pair of hands' quickly discover this not to be the case. The students are there to experience a work situation and ought to be treated as colleagues in the time they are placed. This may paint a rosy picture of the ease of setting up work placements, which is not always the case. The reality seems to be more a case of a minority of employers from industry or headteachers positively requesting students on placement at their establishment, while a majority of placements are arranged only after numerous phone calls have been made and 'begging' letters have been sent.

Before we go on to look at the procedures involved in setting up placement, let us consider our reasons for sending students out into the world of work.

The following is a list of some possible aims for work placement:

- *to enhance learning* – to enable students to deepen their understanding of concepts learned in classroom settings, and to apply skills learned there; i.e. matching theory and practice
- *to motivate* – to make the curriculum more meaningful and significant to students, so improving their levels of academic attainment
- *to promote maturity* – to facilitate students' personal and social development
- *to enhance investigative attitudes* – to enable students to develop their knowledge and understanding of the world of work
- *to expand experience* – to broaden the range of occupations that students are prepared to consider in terms of their personal career planning
- *to give an opportunity for sampling* – to enable students to test their vocational preference before committing themselves to it
- *to prepare* – to help students to acquire skills and knowledge related to a particular occupational area, which they will be ready to apply if they wish to enter employment in that area
- *to anticipate* – to enable students to experience some of the pressures of work so that they will be able to manage the transition to work more easily
- *to open opportunities* – to enable students to establish a relationship with a particular employer which may ultimately lead to the offer of full-time employment

Central to all these aims is the closing of the 'reality gap' between the students' impression of their chosen career and what *actually* happens in the everyday aspects of the job. Work placements are valuable in this respect. Let us look closely at the relationship between the students, the world of work and the college course units/subjects.

Considering our aims stated above, eight of these provide a basis for a curricular frame for work experience.

Curricular frame	Related aims
a Academic subjects	To enhance learning
	To motivate
b Personal and social education	To promote maturity

c   World of work learning   To enhance investigative attitudes
d   Careers education   To expand experience; to give an
                                            opportunity to anticipate
e   Vocational course   To prepare students for the occu-
                                            pational area.

It might be helpful to think of the five curricular frames as points of a
pentagon, with the student at its heart. The aims then become the radii that
link the student to the curricular frames; see Figure 1.

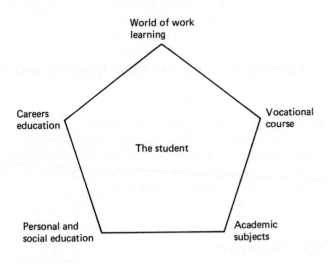

Figure I   Five curricular frames

The workplace supervisor will also carry out the role of assessor. In this
context, thought must be given to the provision of assessment criteria which
are shared by the students, the tutor and the workplace assessor. Appropriate
training and/or liaison will be required to ensure uniformity of understanding
and of standards.

Objectives

We have dealt with overall aims in terms of all types of work placement, but
each course needs to develop specific objectives for particular tasks relevant to
the course. For example,

- in hairdressing – to produce the most appropriate treatment for the
  condition of the hair and the requirements of the client. To understand
  the effects on the hair shaft of chemical substances used in hairdressing.

- in office practice – to produce typewritten and word-processed documents from shorthand and audio dictation. To understand the main types of business organization.
- in electrical installation – to install a domestic ring-main system safely, using correct earthing procedures.
- in motor-vehicle maintenance – to set a plug gap correctly, to install plugs and to join to correct plug-leads.
- in CG 7307 – to prepare a set of lesson notes, indicating lesson objectives, content, and outcomes. To produce appropriate teaching aids.

▶ ## Task 32   Looking at aims and objectives for work placement

Now consider the course for which you are responsible.
1   Look at the list of possible aims for work placement. Decide on at *least* one further *aim* to justify use of work placement as part of your course.
2   Devise at least two principal specific *objectives* peculiar to your course content which could be fulfilled on placement.

Setting up placements

Lecturers and course tutors do not as a rule have enough available time in their administrative and departmental hours to enter into lengthy conversations by telephone or to make half-day visits to employers in industry, personnel officers in hospitals, headteachers in schools or nurseries, or any other work placement. Therefore, a procedure is needed which finds, secures, assesses and arranges placements quickly and in a manner which is both effective and professional. Such a system will have certain key elements. These will include:

- establishing a list of potential placements
- writing a suitable introductory letter
- telephoning confirmations
- visiting the placement
- compiling a statement of intent
- establishing an assessment process
- providing information for students
- problem-solving
- carrying out a terminal review.

In the paragraphs which follow we examine each of these key elements in turn; you may wish to add to, or modify, this list in the light of your own college and employer situation.

1   *Establishing a list of potential placements*
First, compile a list of possible placements relevant to your course. For example, a BTEC National Diploma in Nursery Nursing course tutor would compile a list of nursery schools, centres, infant and junior schools. Headteachers' names and telephone numbers would be recorded alongside. This information should be readily available in the local telephone directory; sometimes colleagues who have used similar placements are often happy to pass on their list of contacts, or the LEA will supply a list. The vital piece of information at this stage is the headteacher's name so that personal contact can be made. If this is not available, telephone the school and ask for the headteacher's name. Similarly, Local Authorities may be accessed for social service establishments. Industrial and commercial organizations can be traced through Yellow Pages or Thompson's Directory. The careers service personnel can also be helpful in identifying likely establishments where young people are treated sympathetically; and this is doubly useful because careers officers will have an eye to the health and safety record of industrial and commercial firms.

2   *Writing a suitable introductory letter*
The next step is to draft a letter to accompany a leaflet of course details to be sent to each headteacher/employer. At this stage you need to be brief but include all relevant details, for example concerning length and timing of placements. This is important, as establishments plan rotas and holidays months ahead.

When writing, stress the reasons for your request for placement of your students. Spell out why the placement is important, what the students will gain, what the employers might gain, and the vocational opportunities which students from the course may eventually access. Try to sound enthusiastic: remember, this is a selling job!

Task 33 Drafting a letter of introduction

Draft a letter introducing yourself and your new course which requires work placements, using the guidelines above.

3   *Telephoning confirmations*
A week after the letter is sent, telephone the headteacher/employer. (Ask for the individual by name: it is always the best possible introduction.) Introduce

yourself, and enquire if he/she has received your letter and course details. Find out if he/she is interested in taking a student or students; and answer any questions or concerns. If the response is positive, arrange a visit within the next few days, or as soon as is possible.

4 Visiting the placement

This may be fairly informal, but you need to project a professional image and be prepared to answer questions and provide as much information as possible in a very short time. The purposes of your visit need to be uppermost in your mind. It is useful to have a checklist in your head; less ideal to take a clipboard and tick things off in an ostentatious manner! Your checklist might include items such as:

- Is the working area safe? (especially on industrial premises – look for unguarded machinery, loose floorcoverings, bad stacking of goods/ equipment, lack of protective clothing, etc.)
- Are workplace personnel, e.g. supervisors, class teachers, secretaries as happy to take students on placement? Resentment may occur if they were not consulted by their managers when the first approach was made. There may be genuine reasons for their reluctance to supervise students; for example, their workloads may be too heavy to take on more duties.
- Will the work experience they are able to provide be appropriate for the students in terms of relating to theory covered in classes? Their future careers? Their personal characteristics? (Here you can begin to consider *particular* students' suitability to different establishments.)
- Are the employers covered by insurance for injury to students and are they willing to take liability, or will public liability need to be brought into play? The employer will need to inform his/her insurers in either case.

If you are satisfied with the establishment in these very general terms, you then need to be certain that the employer is *well prepared* for the student and his/her requirements. Back in college, you will also ensure that the student is equally *well prepared* for the experience. This preparation is the keynote to valuable work experience.

5 Compiling a statement of intent

You will need to set out, in collaboration with the employer, a statement of intent which should include details of all the provision to be made for the student, for example, health and safety considerations, clothing (e.g. whether special protective clothing is necessary), hours of working, meal arrangements, insurance cover and finally a scheme of work to include *all the types of experience* the student will be offered. An arrangement must also be made for the placement supervisory visits. (The number and length of these will depend on the duration of the placement and college policy, but *at least* one visit of sufficient length should be made to each student on placement.)

6   *Establishing an assessment process*

In college, you will of course have developed a scheme of assessment for students on work-placement which takes account of the aims and objectives of the course and any requirements of validating bodies. You will have shared this with colleagues and come to common understanding about how the process is to operate.

At this stage assessment of the student should be discussed with the placement supervisor. He/she should be provided with a sheet which enables the regular recording of attendance, and a sheet which gives a breakdown of skills to be developed on placement. General or generic skills could be assessed first, followed by skills which are to be developed through work on *particular* tasks. Table 17 gives the flavour of what needs to be developed.

7   *Providing information to students*

Once the employer and supervisor have been well prepared, the student needs to receive as much information as possible about what will be expected of him/her on placement. He/she needs to know why placement experience is so

---

TABLE 17   A sample placement report form
EMPLOYERS REPORT

Generic skills
- punctuality
- ability to follow instructions
- relations with manager/supervisor
- relations with customers and clients
- willingness to learn.

(space will be required for the employer to comment and to give examples and illustrations)

Specific skills
These would include operations and competencies relating to specific tasks to be carried out by the trainee such as
- keeping work areas clean
- paying attention to safety rules and procedures
- keeping client records up to date
- understanding the means to access the data-base on client treatments
- charging correct prices
- using the correct invoicing procedure (etc.).

Assessment can be on a numerical or literal scale; but is better when related to examples of competence or lack of skill. Employers should be encouraged to be positive where possible, but to be constructive in suggesting remedial action when students fail to complete tasks satisfactorily at first.

important for personal and social development; and how it relates practice to theory, as well as being vital preparation for the chosen career. Students need to think carefully, and discuss with the tutor, the type of behaviour and dress which will be appropriate for the placement and why. Work over the list of skills to be developed, and a list of practical activities they will be asked to do on placement, so that they come to 'own' them as relevant and valuable. For the duration of a placement, especially one organized over a long period such as a day per week for a term, ideas will be added to these lists as the experiences progress.

8   Problem-solving

Problems may arise when expectations are not lived up to, from both the student and the employer's point of view. It must be made clear at the outset that either party should inform you, the course tutor, if any problems or queries occur. An open door and open telephone line must be always available.

9   Carrying out a terminal review

At the end of the work placement, it is a useful exercise for the students to make a personal assessment in the form of a review. The starting-point for such a terminal review can often be for students and tutors (with work supervisors where practicable) to consider the *extreme* experiences, the best and worst of what happened. A simple questionnaire, with items such as those below, can often start successful discussion:

1   The best experience on placement was . . .
2   The worst experience was . . .
3   The most difficult part of the job was . . .
4   What I think I learned from it was . . .
5   I now wish I had been more . . .

▶ Task 34 Reviewing progress on work placement

Given the ideas in this chapter, plan out the terminal review of work placement for a group of your own students. In particular, consider:
• where the review will take place
• who will be present
• what questions need to be addressed
• where this will fit into the students' further learning.

Following a sequence of Units in which we have looked at student learning in and outside the classroom, it is time to think about the ways in which the outcomes of learning can be recorded.

Unit 9

RECORD-KEEPING

'If the poor only had profiles there would be no difficulty in solving the problem of poverty.'   Oscar Wilde, 1894

Recording progress

The progress of students or pupils has almost always been recorded in some form. Old school record-books catalogue the misdeeds of unrepentant offenders who continued to sin against the system. There are famous school reports which sum up the masters' views of pupils – like the assessment of Winston Churchill: 'Could do better'. A typical school report had a box for the end-of-term exam results, another for position in class and two inches for teacher comment. One of us once had the indignity of reading: History 34%: 28th in class = poor term's work. Later it emerged that the teacher had failed to add in two scores on the exam paper, altering the boxes to 64%, 3rd. The figures were changed but the headteacher ruled that the comment had to remain as the teacher must have meant it! Even to pupils the system was unconvincing. Then later there was the awarding of diplomas and degree certificates for those who succeeded, designed both to certify and advertize that success. But the system logged progress imperfectly, in crude terms: a silhouette rather than a portrait.

Thus it was tempting for profiling to be hailed as the saviour of record-keeping in recent years, after many teachers had become dissatisfied with existing methods of logging success. The need for some form of record-keeping and assessment has rarely been questioned, but methods have changed dramatically over the years.

National curriculum documents are helpful in analysing assessment into four main types:

- *formative* – in that profiling is an ongoing process, informing and helping to mould learning and teaching methods
- *diagnostic* – in that it shows strengths and weaknesses in the students, helping the teacher to compensate where necessary
- *summative* – in that it sums up achievements
- *evaluative* – in that it provides a means of reviewing teaching methods and aiding curriculum development.

Profiling in itself is *not* assessment; it is a form of displaying the *results* of an assessment. Assessment can be a very simple or a very complex process, depending on its purpose. In its simplest form, '*the test*' of knowledge gained over a period of time and prior learning at the outset of a course enables the teacher to:

- find out what the students know
- grade the students by ability
- track the students' progress in terms of different aspects of the course and particular knowledge gained
- discover the effectiveness of particular teaching methods.

Tests and examinations have been replaced on many Further Education courses by 'continuous assessment'. This has meant that keeping very careful records is essential in terms of practical and written work. Not only is it a form of cumulative judgement, it also provides a permanent record of *changes* in the student's performance. In Further Education terms, this means continuing the two-fold method of assessment begun in the high school, i.e. through *Records of Achievement*.

Most younger students now, and all in the future, will come into Further Education with an existing Record of Achievement compiled throughout a school life, the National Record of Achievement. One of the distinctive features of these records is that they ensure student participation both in commenting on the accuracy of the record itself and in producing action plans for their own progress. It might be worthwhile reflecting for a few moments on the reasons why student participation is valuable.

Task 35   Analysing the value of students' own participation in record-keeping

Below is a list of reasons why it may be valuable for students to participate in record-keeping about their own progress. Examine the list, and add at least three more items.

It is helpful for students to participate in record-keeping because:
- they need to know their strengths and weaknesses
- they need to track their progress in each area of study
- they need to receive feedback concerning their whole range of abilities, not simply academic performance
- they need to feel that their own opinion is valued
- they need to feel that they have a right to control their own destiny.

If a critical part of record-keeping and profiling is the action plan, then it is helpful to give some thought to how to implement a system which gives students a chance to draw up such plans. Table 18 suggests the kind of format which is both simple and quick, but also effective in focusing attention.

Task 36   Helping students to formulate action plans

1   Look at the action plan format in Table 18. Adapt this to meet your needs and those of students whom you teach.
2   Having decided on a format for recording action plans, think about how and when you would use the proforma you have developed.
3   Try out the proforma. Adapt it as required.

Action plans can be especially useful because:
- they encourage the auditing of progress
- they encourage realism in the student
- they identify short-term goals
- they are achievable
- they are contractual between student and tutor
- they can be a measure of incremental success
- they are a means of identifying progression
- they are evidence of progress accessible to relevant third parties.

TABLE 18   Student action plans

Get Ahead College of Further Education
STUDENT'S ACTION PLAN

Student's name: Date:

Obstacle	What will I do to overcome this?	What I need to overcome this	Target date	Evaluation strategies

Complete the following:

What I will achieve by .... (date) is ....

....

I'll know when I've done it because ....

....

My plans might be hindered by ....

....

Signed: .... (Student) .... (Tutor)

Assessing students: from knowledge to competence

Unit 7 looked at assessing students' written work. In that Unit two points were made which will bear repetition here:

- In assessing students' work, it is important for tutors to explain clearly, in advance, what is required and how the work is to be judged.
- In making those judgements, tutors need to give feedback to students on what they did well and on how to improve what they did less well.

These two points apply not only to written work, but to all aspects of student activity – in the classroom, on placement or in practical sessions. However, the emphasis of assessing students has shifted from a total reliance on their theoretical knowledge of a subject or their ability to describe what they would do in hypothetical situations, into the business of demonstrating actual abilities. In particular, the emphasis in assessment has moved into the articulation and measurement of competencies – that is, of actual operations required of the employee in the workplace.

As long ago as 1980, the CBI stated that profiles were needed which were meaningful to employers as a whole as well as to college staff and students themselves. But it took another six years before the National Council for Vocational Qualifications was set up to address this problem along with the whole question of comparisons between qualifications. Employers used to be faced with a choice between two candidates armed with either 'O' levels or CSEs, 'A' levels or a BTEC National Diploma. The proliferation of examination boards meant that qualifications could have been awarded by the City and Guilds of London Institute, the RSA Examination Board, Pitman Examinations Institute, the London Chamber of Commerce or the Industry Examination Board! Therefore, an informed choice between candidates with certificates from any of these boards was almost impossible and could have been based upon ignorance of the comparative levels.

GCSE has meant that pre-16 educational achievements can now be more accurately judged relative to other attainments. NCVQ has provided a system of vocational qualifications that has not only standardized them, but has revolutionized their attainment, due to the fact that an NVQ will indicate *competence in employment*. It does this by ensuring that not only is knowledge acquired on a particular course, but that *skills* are developed and the ability to *apply* them at work is tested.

Each NVQ is divided into Units of Competence. Each unit relates to competence in a different area of activity within a job. It will consist of elements of skill, knowledge and understanding and specify the performance required to demonstrate the competence. Units of competence may be simple, e.g. using a telephone, or very complex, e.g. changing a gearbox. This all depends on the nature of the qualification. Units of Competence in turn make up Elements of Competence such as the one in Table 19. Note the detailed performance criteria.

Therefore it can be seen that the measurement of competencies by an assessor is more objective in that the criteria are very clearly defined; personal bias is less likely to impinge on the assessment. Nevertheless, the assessment of competence can still be both difficult and somewhat ambiguous. At the lowest levels, competencies can be simple functions: a student can perform, or not, as the case may be. But it is far harder to judge criteria like performance criterion (f) in Table 19. How can one be sure of customer goodwill or the opposite? It *may* be obvious, but it may be open to interpretation.

This system of assessment and record-keeping in terms of a set of criteria is familiar to those teachers in further education dealing with students taking

TABLE 19   Some competencies examined

NVQ Title – *Financial Services (Building Societies) Level II*
Unit 1   Provide information and advice and promote products and services to customers.

Element 11   Inform customers about products and services on request.

Range of variables to which the element applies.

Products:
Investment – instant access, higher rate, notice accounts, regular savings.
Lending – mortgages, further advances, personal secured loans, unsecured loans, credit cards.
Insurance – property, personal, travel.
Services – foreign currency, traveller's cheques, credit card, share dealing.
Customers – minors, teenagers, 16+, middle-aged, pensioners, professional contacts,
                     companies, non-resident groups.

Performance criteria

(a)   Features, advantages and benefits of services sufficient to the customer's
        request are described clearly and accurately.   ☐

(b)   Example calculations are correct.   ☐

(c)   Appropriate information is accessed from available resources (incl. viewdata).   ☐

(d)   Information requests outside the responsibility of the job holder are passed
        on to an appropriate authority promptly and accurately.   ☐

(e)   Customers are acknowledged promptly and treated politely.   ☐

(f)   Customers are treated in a manner which promotes good will.   ☐

Elements of Competence Achieved

Assessor   Noted by
Endorsement   Candidate

(NCVQ 1990, p. 8)

BTEC, City and Guilds, RSA, PEI and LCCIEB courses. BTEC students in particular have long been tested on *common skills*, that is, transferable skills of e.g. communication using information technology, working with others, etc. In all these courses, too, there has always been an emphasis on the distinction between actual learning and topics covered. The testing of that knowledge has been possible through *practical* experience which all of these courses provide. The placement supervisors and/or assessors in college in mock workshops, salons etc., are able to keep detailed records of the students' achievements, relevant to the particular experiences available. For example, a student on a BTEC National Diploma in Caring Services (Nursery Nursing) on a nursery-school work placement could have records kept on his/her performance in schools, of the kind shown in Table 20.

TABLE 20   Sample record sheet: Hotstuff College
BTEC NATIONAL DIPLOMA IN (CARING SERVICES)

Report of Practical Placement in the   (Term)   (Year)

STUDENT'S NAME: ....   ESTABLISHMENT: ....

DATES OF PLACEMENT: ....

....

Please comment on the student's level of competency during the time spent with you according to the headings given. If you want to make further comments, please use the additional spaces. Your report and comments will be discussed with the student and will form part of their assessment. Your co-operation is, therefore, greatly appreciated.

	LEVEL OF COMPETENCY					
	Please tick appropriate box					
	Very good	Good	Average	Satis-factory	Poor	Additional comments
Professionalism Student's attitude to and relationship with: – children						
– staff						
– parents						
– student's level of initiative						
– timekeeping						

– reliability						
– response to individual child's needs						
– response to group needs of children						
– personal presentation/appearance						
– respect of confidentiality						
Student's communication skills Student communicated with: – different age groups of children						
– parents						
– staff						
– other professionals						

	Please tick appropriate box					
	Al-ways	Usually	Some-times	Seldom	Never	Additional comments
Student's observational skills Student observed: – developmental patterns and stages within age groups of children						
– Experienced staff communicate with the child/children						
– parents' communication with own and other children						
– interaction between children						
Student's areas of responsibility The student: – followed appropriate lines of communication						
– observed health and safety practices						

– observed and applied equal opportunities					

Placement supervisor
Signature: .... Date: ....
Designation: ....

Discussion with Course Co-ordinator/Tutor and student in tutorial.

Course Co-ordinator/Tutor
Signature: .... Date: ....

Student
Signature: .... Date: ....

Developing your own profiling system

Finally in this Unit we look at the steps that a tutor will need to take in order to develop a profiling system of his or her own, and we discuss some criteria for judging the system's effectiveness. A good profiling system probably depends, as we have suggested in other Units, on students maintaining personal logbooks. The data collected by the student and contained in such a logbook would include, for example:

- work experience and unpaid jobs
- tv programmes, films or videos enjoyed
- creative work
- people the student had met or had important conversations with
- hobbies, clubs etc.
- visits out of college
- sports he/she had taken part in
- activities in groups
- writing – letters/essays
- new things learned and subjects studied
- equipment and machinery used
- projects completed
- link or further education courses
- books read
- new skills learned
- living away from home – residential experience.

Task 37   Planning the contents of the student's logbook

Given the ideas above, what else would you want students to include in the personal logbooks?

In addition to what students themselves record, the student's record of achievement needs to focus on these abilities and skills in students:

- the student's knowledge – of facts, information
- the student's practical skills and competencies
- the student's understanding – of concepts and processes
- the student's ability to analyse, examine and question data
- the student's ability to form hypotheses
- the student's creativity and imagination
- the student's aesthetic appreciation
- the student's cross-curricular and common skills
- the student's social skills
- the student's activities and experiences in college and outside.

Over a period of time the sequence of events required for effective profiling is likely to contain the following steps:

| Log book kept by student | ⟶ | Review by student/tutor | ⟶ | Periodic progress report | ⟶ | Final report |

Finally, some thoughts about the fundamental content of good records of achievement. Good records:

- bring together assessment and learning
- link process with outcome
- involve both tutors and students
- lead to guidance, advice or counselling when needed
- emphasize success.

From examining some criteria for evaluation and good record-keeping we move on to the rather broader issue of defining and seeking to pursue quality in Further Education courses.

Unit 10

MONITORING QUALITY

Defining quality

Quality in education is a difficult concept. Even before we can examine it we need to define what we mean. A good place to begin might be to explore what we would mean if we were to describe a course as 'of good quality'.

Task 38   Exploring the meaning of quality

1   Imagine you have been asked by your line manager to say what makes your course/your department's courses 'of good quality'. What factors would you list?
2   What quality indicators don't apply to your/your department's course, but would be things you would add in ideal circumstances?

Now you will have generated a list which begins to define the concept of quality. It will probably include items such as these, though the list is for example only and is not exhaustive:

- good relationships between students and tutors
- comfortable peer-group relationships within the student group
- committed tutorial support by staff
- good relations with work-placement providers
- easy discipline in and beyond college
- student commitment to classwork and homework

- interesting and varied approaches to teaching method
- motivation and enthusiasm by tutors and students
- effective mastering of academic work by students
- high standards of practical work on placement
- good examination results
- a high post-qualifying rate of employment for students
- student satisfaction with the course both during it and in retrospect.

So the quality of a course can be judged, it is suggested, by reference to identifiable (even if not easily measured) criteria. But these criteria – however long the list is – may turn out to be rather parochial in their attempt to illustrate and amplify the notion of quality. For example, we have not explored the issue of quality in relation to the role of the tutor, itself capable of more detailed examination. Nor have we opened up the wider context of quality as exemplified by efficiency or cost effectiveness, an increasingly important political dimension in education. Nor, indeed, have we paid any attention to quality as applied to an institution within which a course or cluster of courses operates.

So how can quality be adequately defined and effectively monitored? It is such a large issue that a book like this can do no more than select a few key issues for examination and alert the reader of the need to pursue the matter further. In a sense, the whole of this book is about the quality of teaching performance. In this Unit we shall look at typical institutional approaches to monitoring quality – through mission statements and course review. We will then move on to review the use of performance indicators. Finally, we will apply these procedures back to the individual course and course tutor to see what they have to tell us about personal professional performance and development.

Quality through mission

From an institutional point of view, the yardstick against which many colleges try to define and then monitor quality is to be found in the form of a mission statement. These mission statements tend to be quite short, perhaps one or two sides of A4. They attempt to set out:

- what the college sees as its role (e.g. in the local educational context)
- where it places its present strengths
- what developments it would like to implement.

Sometimes such mission statements may attempt to show how the aspirations can be achieved, or by whom, or to describe time-scales; but these are not strictly necessary within the statement itself. Mission statements attempt to paint the broad canvas of institutional aspiration, and do not fill in the fine detail of the planning.

Task 39   Exploring your college's mission statement

1   Do you know what your college's mission statement says? Do you have a copy? If so, do you ever consult it to compare its macro-level aspiration against what you are trying to achieve?
2   If you do have a copy of the mission statement, or can obtain one, go through it in detail and try to analyse and list where your work flows into, and from, its content.
3   If there is no mission statement in your institution, write one. Include what you think it ought to contain.
4   If possible, ask a colleague to try to write a mission statement (you could use this as an in-service activity for course or department staff). Compare your statement with those of your colleagues.

Mission statements are useful as the broad guideline and policy frameworks within which institutions function. They vary in quality, and it may be worthwhile pausing for a moment to look at some characteristics of good mission statements, and some of the things that may epitomize weaker mission statements. These are set out in Table 21.

TABLE 21   Characteristics of good, and weak, institutional mission statements

Good factors	Weak factors
Brief, business-like	Overly long, obscure
Expressed in clear English	Rhetorical, jargonistic
Well laid out	Poorly presented
Related to reality	Too ambitious
Negotiated with all staff	Compiled by senior management
Achievable	Wedded to philosophy, not practice
Identifying clear targets	Platitudinous
Identifying intermediate stages in success	Lacking indications of progress
Putting clients at the centre	Putting the institution at the centre
Relating the institution to its context	Ignoring the contextual issues

Performance indicators

The mission statement sets out some of the qualitative goals which an institution espouses. But the process of measuring the extent to which they are being achieved brings us to the need to identify and agree on performance indicators. Performance indicators are those factors which can be used to help determine whether institutional goals are being met. Since the Audit Commission report, *NAFE in practice* (HMI 1987), and the 1988 Education Reform Act, much has changed in FE and a greatly increased pressure has been applied to colleges to produce measures of accountability. These measures can be used sensibly, or like the proverbial blunt instrument, so it is important both to understand them and to view them in context. The context will include the governmental and LEA policies, the institutional mission statement or its equivalent, institutional review procedures, and the degree to which individual tutors and students feel part of the accountability and monitoring process.

What kind of performance indicators can be used to measure whether an institution is achieving the ideals of its mission statement? Let us simply list half a dozen to give the flavour:

- student–staff ratios
- examination success rates
- cost effectiveness of courses
- student post-course employment rates
- student satisfaction with their courses
- pastoral and personal support of students

All of these have been widely used by colleges as performance indicators to measure quality. Yet while each has its purpose, each is also open to ambiguity, interpretation or even misuse.

It may be generally supposed that, for courses to be efficient, a student–staff ratio in the region of 13:1 needs to be achieved. The student-staff ratio is calculated by a formula, a simplified version of which is as follows:

$$\text{SSR} = \frac{\text{average class size} \times \text{average lecturer-hours}}{\text{average student hours}}$$

Using this formula, a class of 16 students meeting for 30 hours a week might have an SSR of $(16 \times 21)/30 = 12.6{:}1$; but quite a small shift of hours down to 28 per week makes the class viable in economic terms: $\text{SSR} = 13.5{:}1$. However, the raw statistic does not address a central question: what is the curriculum effect on students of the loss of two hours' teaching, and what will go?

Similarly, the examination success rate of a course may be measured at 58.6 per cent: rather a modest score, one might think. But the specific course might have a national pass rate of 41.2 per cent, which would make the college's performance fairly good.

Cost effectiveness could mean that the cluster of courses in a given department could be put on at £125 per FTE student, £17 per head cheaper than last year. In context, though, this does not help the casual reader of the statistic to understand whether savings are due to acceptable cost-cutting through wise use of discounts on equipment purchases, or because an educational visit has been jettisoned to save money.

Students in Downbeat College may have a 70 per cent employment rate after successful completion of courses, while in Upmarket College this may be 83 per cent. But in Downbeat Borough the overall unemployment rate may be 22 per cent, while in Upmarket Town it may be only 3 per cent. *In context* Downbeat's record would be more than commendable.

These and many other variables and unknowns warn us against the unsophisticated use of performance indicators, and particularly of those where an apparently indisputable, and easily comparable, numerical value may be assigned to the measure.

By contrast, student satisfaction with courses is not numerical, is more difficult to explore – and more time-consuming to analyse. Qualitatively, though, this performance indicator may be more useful, and have more real meaning, than the apparently 'accurate' statistics. The same would hold true of a college's pastoral and support system: a good system is probably a useful performance indicator, but to define and assess 'goodness' here is more difficult – and so to many people less attractive – than a rapid statistical measurement.

So our rapid review of performance indicators leads us to weigh the pros and cons against appropriate contextual data. In *context*, and where a wide range of *both* quantitative and qualitative measures are used, they are an increasingly important way of monitoring college performance and carrying out proper processes of accountability. The need to do this is emphasized by recent Government documents such as DES 1991.

Of course, these examples given have been at an institutional level, while this book is mainly about individual tutors and courses, or about sharing of perceptions and skills by groups of staff up to a department level. So the next task is to apply these insights to the course level of operation in the task that follows.

▶ **Task 40   Identifying performance indicators in your course**

1   What range of
(a)   quantitative and
(b)   qualitative
data do you think would be appropriate to collect to shed light on your course(s)?
2   Make a list of about five or six items relating to both (a) and (b) above.
3   For each of the ten or so performance indicators identified, suggest how you might carry out the measurement or monitoring required.
4   If possible, persuade a colleague to carry out the same exercise independently. Compare your lists, and conflate or amend them as you see fit.
(N.B. This would be a good exercise to be carried out by a course or department team.)

▶ **Task 41   Monitoring your course through performance indicators**

1   Now that you have identified appropriate performance indicators for your course, undertake an evaluation of your course using these as the evidence.
2   When all the evidence is collected, tease out the conclusions you would draw.
3   What action will you take as a result of this monitoring exercise?

Performance indicators are probably best deployed in institutions where all staff have had the opportunity to contribute to the debate about what is appropriate evidence of quality. In individual colleges there are usually course review procedures at various levels which institutionalize the process of examining quality. They are important, but are only one approach to quality control and assurance. At present LEAs need to agree with their constituent colleges the basis on which the monitoring takes place at the LEA level through performance indicators. Such indicators will allow college, departments, course leaders and even individual tutors to undertake self-monitoring. Any internal monitoring or external monitoring, e.g. by the LEA advisers or Her Majesty's Inspectors will need to build on, and take account of, this self-monitoring process. When new legislation comes on stream in April 1993 accountability will still be required but the LEA role will diminish.

Quality control

So far in this Unit we have attempted if not actually to *define* quality, at least to *refine* precisely what factors go to make up a 'course of quality', and to see what kinds of monitoring activity we can draw out of objective evidence which can illuminate professional judgements made in their proper contexts. We have seen that, in that sense, quality permeates all levels of college life, from the individual tutor or student to the institutional performance. It has been indicated that all staff need a stake in institutional monitoring; and all students need to identify with the process of course and departmental monitoring. There need to be systems of recording and reporting on quality at all levels. This reporting and recording on quality applies not just to the academic areas of courses, but to the practical and work placements, too. This kind of approach is sometimes now known in the jargon as total quality management or just TQM. Table 22 attempts to set out some marks of quality for work placements.

TABLE 22   Quality indicators in work placement and experience

The following factors are highlighted by HMI (1990) *Education observed: work-based learning in FE*

- Realistic work activities in a real or well-simulated environment
- Provision of challenging tasks
- Opportunities to display organizational skills, leadership, communication and confidence
- A degree of pressure resulting from actual situations
- Opportunities to supervise other students or clients
- Need for team-work
- Need to meet deadlines or cost-limits
- Real responsibility for students
- High standards of performance

Though this is not the place to pursue the argument, it should be noted that not only academic staff and work placement supervisors, but support staff too, need to be committed to, and involved in, the monitoring of quality with respect to their roles through proper performance indicators: the experience of a student during a course may be a hypothetical issue if the administrative assistant who deals with his/her attempted enrolment is unwelcoming!

Perhaps it would be helpful to end this Unit – which by the very nature of such a wide-ranging and complicated issue, can do no more than skim the surface – by looking at the attitude of the professional towards quality control.

Historically, the role of HMI in particular has been associated with tension, insecurity and resentment. This attitude by teaching staff is entirely un-derstandable (and occasional HMIs may even have helped to cause it!) – but it does not represent a sensible approach to external monitoring. More recently, government pressure to treat education more like a business, with overtones of profitability and efficiency, has caused more tremors in professionals who prefer to define their business and their individual roles in language that reflects educational ideals without reference to cost. Both contain degrees of truth; and documents like *NAFE in practice* have helped to draw the two perspectives closer. Monitoring quality *should* be seen by professionals as a positive process that enhances performance and role, rather than one which detracts from it. For this reason this Unit ends with a very positive Task.

▶ ## Task 42   Assessing what is positive about monitoring

List the good reasons why monitoring of quality should be welcomed by colleagues, individual tutors and students.

The mark of quality

For completeness, it ought to be noted that there is currently a move to establish a 'kite mark' system for colleges known as British Standard (BS) 5750. In brief, colleges would need to satisfy specific quality-control proced-ures. Subject to this, courses would have the BS 5750 'seal of approval'. A discussion of this is outside the scope of this book (it does, for example, have cost implications for colleges, and BS 5750 is a commercial rather than an educational standard). The very existence of this scheme is, however, indica-tive of a trend in quality assurance.

Conclusion

You have now reached the half-way stage in the book: ten Units completed. The emphasis so far has been on creating the right ethos, on teaching and learning strategies, on assessment and on quality. The next three Units move the spotlight onto students' specific needs and onto specific groups of students.

Unit 11

TEACHING ADULT STUDENTS

There are just under a million adult students following courses in FE colleges and they tend to be found in one of two strategic contexts. Either the college will have a specialist adult education provision of some kind (a special course of general education, an advice centre, a specific department and so on), or adult students will appear in a range of courses alongside post-16 young people. Indeed, the two approaches are not mutually exclusive; but for the purposes of this Unit it will probably be easier to examine the two separate contexts as well as looking at more general skills for teaching adults.

Adult students come to college with a wide range of attitudes, concerns and motivations. These students are probably a typical cross-section:

> Jane: 'I'm fifty four, and I spend a lot of time at home on my own. I've always been interested in a range of things – embroidery, acquiring a bit of each foreign language when I've been going abroad to various places, local and family history. I like to try new things, too, like carpentry and upholstery. So several years ago I thought I'd see what the local college had to offer by way of part-time courses. I wanted a bit of social contact, too. At first I signed up for something I was good at, which was a mistake really because I didn't learn much. Now I do something every year . . . '

> Harry: 'I was out of work six months, and then I got a leaflet through the door. It said "Why not use your spare time to learn something useful?" So I joined up on a First Aid class. I was very unhappy about going along on the first day; well, I knew this place

thirty years ago, when you had to be clever to go here from school and the staff were very strict. But it's changed a lot, and First Aid helped me get a part-time job.'

Freda: 'I missed out on my education, you know. When I was a girl, my father couldn't see the point. My brothers went out to work at the first opportunity and I was left at home to do the chores while mother earned too. I've always felt cheated, so I decided rather late in life to make up for lost time. The course allows you to 'pick and mix' 'A' levels – I'm doing sociology and modern history this year, and last year I got a 'B' in English. If possible I'm going the whole hog, so when I've passed this lot I'm going for an Open University degree.'

Richard: 'I'm a bank employee and I come here in the evenings, two nights a week for two years. I'm taking banking qualifications. The course is hard and some of it seems pretty pointless. But I want to manage my own branch eventually so this is one chore I have to get out of the way . . . '

Jacquie: 'My children have gone to school now, so I can just about squeeze in a full-time course; my mum helps me a lot by picking up the kids from school. I'm training as a nursery nurse. Yes, it was a bit strange sitting in class with a lot of sixteen-year-olds at first. But I'm not old-fashioned and we get on just fine . . . '

Motivation and purpose for attending college are important pointers to how adult students expect and need to be taught. For them, time in the out-of-college world can be short and full of conflicting demands, and they are likely to value very task-orientated college sessions and work experiences. From the tutor's point of view, understanding the perspective of adult students is a crucial starting-point in teaching them effectively.

Task 43   Understanding the adult student's viewpoint

1   Select two adult students in your course/department and arrange to talk to them in-depth quite informally. Explain why you are asking them to help you in this way and assure them of the confidentiality of their responses.

2   Try to explore their motivations, purposes, thoughts and feelings about their college experience. Pre-determine your main questions (Table 23 may help you), but also be prepared to follow any leads they may give you.

TABLE 23   Eliciting the adult student's viewpoint: some possible questions to discuss

1   How did you first become aware of the course you are now following?
2   What were the most important factors that motivated you to gain a place on the course?
3   What do you hope to do with the knowledge/skills/qualification(s) you gain from the course?
4   What were your first impressions of the college and of the course?
5   Have these first impressions been modified in any way? How?
6   Are the teaching and learning methods you have encountered on the course what you expected? If not, how do they differ?
7   If this course were offered to adult students only, how would you expect it to differ from its present form?
8   Apart from knowledge, skills and qualifications, what other benefits have you gained from the course? (Probe for social gains, for evidence of changed feelings and attitude outside college, etc.)
9   What are the main drawbacks to being an adult student?
10   What could be changed about the course/college to make it more attractive to adult students?

Teaching adults and young students together

As we have seen, adults and young students are often taught side by side, especially on GCSE/GCE programmes and on courses leading to initial vocational qualifications. This may mean that one's *whole* approach to the course needs to be modified since it is almost always inappropriate to discriminate between adult and young students in any course activity. A good way to think positively about course adaptation is to make a list of the strengths and weaknesses such a mixed group of students may exhibit.

Task 44   Examining the strengths and weaknesses of mixed-age classes

1   Make a list of all the positive advantages and strengths which mixed classes might possess.
2   Make a similar list of the disadvantages which you can see in mixed-age classes. In each case use the following pointers to get you started.

Possible advantages/strengths
- Adult students can be very committed and enthusiastic.
- Experiences brought by adult students can be valuable, and are shared.
- Mature behaviour steadies some of the excitable youngsters.
- Adult students are often helpful on a pastoral level to the younger ones.
-
-
-

Possible disadvantages/weaknesses
- Some of the formal course content is inevitably pitched at too low a level for adults.
- Some adult students 'act young' in unhelpful ways.
- Some adult students can be distracted by domestic issues and disturb other students.
- There is a tendency to use the adults as leaders, so the younger students lose out.
-
-
-

Provision aimed mainly at adult students

Many colleges have some areas of provision which are accessed mainly by adult students. These take various forms. Traditionally GCSE/GCE courses have been in this mould in colleges, but Open Tech, flexi-study, open learning, access programmes and courses for the unemployed have become common additions and alternatives. HMI discovered that many colleges are not effective in providing for adults, and these were some of the reasons:

- course fees were too high
- timing of provision was inappropriate
- staff-in-charge were insufficiently senior to bring about co-operation from providing departments
- students were not consulted enough about the nature of the provision
- staff-in-charge were out of touch with students and/or the community
- many tutors were not qualified as teachers
- many tutors were on part-time contracts
- teaching methods were inappropriate
- ethos or ambience of many colleges was unsuitable
- there was lack of provision (inadequate refectories, no creche, etc).

Task 45   Providing for courses aimed at adult students

1   What courses are there in your college which are aimed mainly/exclusively at adult students?
2   Using the problems outlined by HMI (listed above), examine the effectiveness of the college's provision.
3   In your own area of work, what could be done to attract and provide for adult students?

Teaching, learning and adult students

So far in this Unit it has been implied that adult students' needs should be considered quite specifically and separately when colleges are planning course provision and when tutors are considering teaching and learning strategies. For the remainder of the Unit the emphasis will be on teaching and learning methods and the adult student. Clearly, what has been said so far implies that a tutor should have a plan for dealing with adult students. This plan would probably include the following stages:

- making sure that course information and advertizing sets out clearly the demands of the course, and the nature of its teaching and learning styles
- exploring at the interview stage with adult students their perceptions, motivations and purposes
- devising activities during induction or early in the life of the course to build confidence in adult students through initial success (the section of Unit 3 on study skills will give additional help)
- ensuring that, wherever possible, adult students can work in ways which are practically and academically appropriate (without discriminating against younger students in the class)
- using, without exploiting, the real strengths of adult students (already identified in this Unit); and being aware of, and compensating for, any disadvantages inherent in 'mixed-age' classes
- providing appropriate guidance and counselling strategies with adult students
- providing language support if required.

Table 24 sets out some possible pointers to the successful integration of adult students into the work and life of an FE college.

One particularly sensitive area when dealing with adult students is that of written course work. Many adult students are not used to putting their thoughts on paper; and most have not done so for a long time. The handling of

TABLE 24   Some possible pointers to successful integration of adult students into the FE college

Successful courses will probably . . .

- establish marketing procedures geared to adult students' likely needs
- have an advice centre with a drop-in facility
- provide access courses
- provide suitable catering, creche and similar facilities
- consult adult students about the teaching/learning needs
- employ experienced staff to lead and contribute to classes for adults
- provide good study facilities in college – in the library, computer area
- time courses to suit adult study-patterns
- exploit open learning and flexible learning possibilities
- modularize courses
- use staff who have an appropriate manner for teaching adults
- give staff involved with adult students a high profile
- forge links with local employers who may supply/employ students
- create an appropriate learning environment for adult learning
- create a suitable college ethos for adult learning
- promote the profile of adult learning achievement, e.g. through the local press
- provide through-routes from elementary to more advanced courses
- train local employers to identify potential course opportunities
- be prepared to provide tuition off-site where appropriate
- meet minority, specialist or specific local needs.

this process is often a crucial factor in how comfortable an adult student feels in an FE course. The worst scenarios would be like the one described below (and while it would be equally bad in the context of a course for post-16s, they may be less intolerant of it):

'The written work was set as homework on Thursday, and had to be in on Friday. It was a traditional essay, and we had the title dictated to us in class without further guidance. All this took place at the very end of the lecture so there was no time to ask questions. I didn't know how much to write so I did about eight pages. It took till midnight. We got the essays back two weeks later. They were given out in class, and the teacher went through the errors in each one publicly. I felt pretty sick waiting for my turn. I suppose it wasn't too bad in the end; two wrong spellings and some criticism of style – but the content seemed satisfactory. Then, when they were given back, my essay only had 6/10 on it, which surprised me. The tutor had written "too long" in the margin but that was all. I wasn't sure whether this was a good result or not for this tutor.'

Task 46   Devising a strategy for dealing with adult students' written work

1   Draw up a positive strategy for dealing with the written work of adult (and other?) students in your class.
2   Discuss this strategy with colleagues. Where appropriate, amend and implement it.

Teaching styles for adults need careful thought. It is not that adult students need *different* teaching styles, but rather that the *balance* may be different. Sixteen-year-olds may welcome a larger proportion of didactic learning than adults do; but all the alternative strategies that are effective with young students should be useful with adults:

- discussion
- group work
- projects
- presentations by the students themselves
- practical exercises
- simulation
- role playing.

Adult students may be more self-conscious; and, having been away from the classroom for a while, they may need to be coached initially in these methods of learning. Adult students may not realize at first *how* to learn from these techniques and the tutor must always be sensitive to this.

Finally, it is perhaps worth drawing attention to the reluctance of some tutors to teach adults. Many teachers find their confidence and sense of authority diminished by the presence of adults in the classes. For these tutors it is important to learn that both student and tutor have individual experiences, personalities and value. Each needs to respect the other. The same is always true in the classroom with students or pupils of any age. Understanding that is part of each tutor's professionalism and integrity.

Unit 12

GIVING VOCATIONAL GUIDANCE TO STUDENTS

'Careers education and guidance have a vital contribution to make to education as a whole in our schools and colleges.'
('Working Together for a Better Future', DES/DOE/Welsh Office, 1987)

Exploring the nature of vocational guidance

A decade or two ago careers education or vocational guidance in schools and Further Education colleges was a limited affair, perhaps involving a few visits to local firms and an interview with a careers officer. These days it is generally accepted that every student has an entitlement to careers education, guidance and counselling, which play a vital role in preparation for adult life. The definitions of these activities have been extended. A 'career' does not refer only to employment, paid or unpaid, and unemployment, but a way through life. Vocational advice is provided in an ongoing process throughout school and college lives, to highlight opportunities available to help young people plan for the future, not only in educational terms as a means to an end (i.e. a particular job) but to help them take their place as adults in society. This is shown diagrammatically in Figure 2.

It is with this broad brief in mind that we as college tutors need to advise our students. We need to provide them with activities which aim to help them to make the right choices and help them through the transition of their careers.

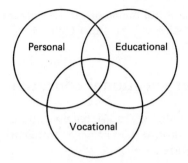

Figure 2   A total learning experience

Students are individuals, and as such need individual guidance in a continual process in which the personal, educational and vocational aspects merge. Consider, then, the aims of vocational advice.

Task 47   Identifying the aims of vocational guidance

Below is a list of possible aims; try to add at least two *more* aims.
The aims of vocational education and guidance are:
- to help students assess their own strengths, abilities and weaknesses and gain 'self-awareness'
- to help students gain a greater understanding of personal relationships and social responsibility
- to assist students in seeing their role in society, the world of work and in their own community
- to develop an awareness of the role and importance of industry in society
- to help students develop skills and attitudes and gain underpinning knowledge which will give them confidence and help them achieve success
- to assist students with their own personal *action plans*
- to help students develop reasoned decision-making skills
- to assist students in developing transition skills
- to make students aware of opportunities available to them and of the demands they make and rewards they offer
- to encourage students to look beyond stereotypes and consider a wide variety of options
-
-
-

Equal opportunity is a central theme of careers guidance, as we need to focus on the potential of *all* students. See also Unit 13.

The objectives of vocational education

Given the broader definition of vocational education, what are the objectives which one might, as a tutor, seek to achieve through it? Perhaps they fall quite neatly into three categories.

1   Relationships
This heading implies the need to facilitate learning about personal relationships, to help students become aware of their own feelings and those of others. This we can do by developing a group structure where individuals support each other and develop an understanding of teamwork and competition. In this way, the group is helped towards better social competence; individual problems can be addressed; students begin to take responsibility for their own decisions.

2   The worlds of work and higher education
Students need to be prepared for higher education or a job. To do this they need to be aware of the opportunities available and necessary qualifications or training required. Liaison and co-operation with the careers officer assigned to the college can be helpful here. The students need to be made aware of the economic situation and how this affects future employers (including educational institutions) as well as how companies work and how industry operates. Information concerning unions and other powerful influences (e.g. TUC, CBI, multi-nationals) needs to be provided. Another important issue is health and safety at work.

3   Social life
Students must become aware of different lifestyles and in particular how work can affect our lives. Leisure activities need to be considered and ideas developed. We need to stress the importance of good relationships between colleagues at work, and rights and responsibilities regarding yourself and other people at work. In particular, students need to begin to develop strategies for coping with change in this fast-moving world and changing scenes in industry and education. Transitions require positive strategies. Consider, for example, the following as aids to transition:

- developing opportunity selling skills
- developing skills of choosing and determining priorities

- developing job-seeking skills
  - application forms
  - letters of application
  - selection tests
  - self-presentation
  - interviews
- personal finance and budgeting
- transition from college to work/higher education – differences, responsibilities, relationships, expectations.

Meeting the objectives of vocational education

In the previous section we looked at some of the possible objectives of our broadly defined scheme of vocational education. For tutors in colleges a key consideration is: how can these objectives be met? A TVEI document (1990a) offers some illuminating thoughts on this.

The TVEI work suggests that a series of core conditions need to be fulfilled for this to happen, bearing in mind that Further Education teachers see themselves as facilitators rather than instructors. These conditions relate to the atmosphere created by tutors:

- *respect* – being willing to listen, not judge
- *empathy* – trying to appreciate how students feel and being able to show your understanding
- *genuineness* – being as natural as possible, 'being yourself' when appropriate.

Students need to feel they can trust you, as tutor, to rely on your advice. This advice can be offered in a variety of different ways:

- by informing
- by advising
- by counselling
- by structuring
- by learning
- by assessing
- by advocating
- by referring.

As a tutor it is necessary to cultivate particular skills oneself. These include:

- listening skills
- questioning skills

- feedback skills
- confronting skills
- skills in using and interpreting non-verbal communication.

Some of these skills are worth considering in greater detail; Table 25 helps to explore the dimensions of these skills in a little more detail.

TABLE 25	Component skills in offering vocational education and guidance
Skill	*Some component factors*
Informing	Providing information which is • accurate • up to date • accessible • objective Word processing, information retrieval
Advising	Providing advice which • is objective • suggests alternatives • is well informed • allows students thinking-time • does not impose a view or course of action
Counselling	Providing counselling which • leads to reflection • promotes student self-reliance
Structuring learning	Providing styles of learning which • promote decision-making skills • encourage maturity • promote empathy and imagination
Assessing	Providing assessment structures which • help students to be realistic about their own achievements • include self-assessment • result in Records of Achievement
Advocating	Providing help through negotiation by • arranging placements • consulting with higher-education institutions on behalf of a student

Referring	Providing contacts with specialist agencies when your own ability to assist ceases, e.g.
	• staff of other departments
	• careers staff
	• employers

Personal skills	
Listening skills	• Being receptive; hearing overt and covert messages
Questioning skills	• Using open-ended questions; helping students to refine the issue
Feedback skills	• Reflecting back what is said so that the student can react to it
Confronting skills	• Helping students to think about consequences
Skills in non-verbal communication	• Carefully observing the students' non-verbal messages and being aware of your own

Planning vocational education and guidance

Good managers maintain diaries and keep year-planners, and this is no less valuable a technique in structuring vocational guidance within the college than it is for other activities. Table 26 gives an example of a possible calendar of activities for a tutor who is monitoring vocational education of a group of young students on a care course run over a traditional academic year.

TABLE 26   A sample year-planner for promoting vocational education and guidance

SEPTEMBER
• Check examination results for possible changes in plan for some students, e.g. some students may require maths GCSE for entry into higher education and may be able to arrange a re-sit or a flexible learning programme within your college to retake it the following year.
• Organize a set of new record-sheets for new students.
• Make sure that there is adequate information available in the library in terms of prospectus application forms, etc.

OCTOBER
• Provide counselling for students who have not decided on career moves – higher education/employment.
• Fill in reports on University/Polytechnic/College applicants.

NOVEMBER
- Follow up destinations of student leavers in the summer term for your records.

JANUARY
- Arrange interviews with careers officer for first-year students.

FEBRUARY
- Arrange for a Grants Officer from the LEA to talk to the students and parents about awards for higher education/Further Education.

MAY
- Arrange link courses with Further Education or work experience for the post-examination weeks.
- Ensure that all leavers have seen the careers officer and made arrangements for their future careers in higher education/employment.
- Draft references for the students in anticipation of request from higher education/employers.

JUNE
- Make arrangements for the local advisory officer to talk to the students about the information service for advanced further and higher education.
- Liaise with the careers officer to organize talks to the students on applications to higher education, etc.
- Complete summative records on students using your own and colleagues' records.
- Make sure that students' CVs and Records of Achievement are complete.

Task 48   Planning the key events in vocational education

With the help of Table 26, devise your own year-planner to support your programme of vocational education and guidance, operating within the context of your own course, students and programme timing.

Helping students find an acceptable place, occupation and style in life is a very important part of the tutor's total role and responsibility. All students need this help, though some minority groups may have particular needs. It is to the specific needs of those minorities to which we turn in the next Unit.

Unit 13

SUSTAINING EQUAL OPPORTUNITIES AND MEETING SPECIAL EDUCATIONAL NEEDS

Equal opportunities: some gender issues

It is salutary to think that even thirty years ago many FE colleges might have been technical institutions at which female students would have been a notable rarity. Indeed, the overwhelming population of these colleges would have been white males – a very different situation from the one which now pertains in most inner cities, at any rate. Yet it would be a mistake to believe that all discrimination has been eliminated from the FE system or that equal opportunities prevail without exception in all institutions or vocational courses covered by Further Education.

In this Unit we aim to give only some basic ideas and guidance on these matters: there is not space in a general teaching skills manual to deal with the more detailed issues. However, readers may wish to follow up the leads provided in the bibliography. The Unit begins by looking at equal opportunities for women.

▶ Task 49   Analysing the college's approach to equal opportunities

1   In your college is there an equal opportunities policy? If so, is it written down, widely disseminated and accessible?
2   If some of the answers to (1) are negative, try to account for this.
3   In practical terms, how does the college policy (or lack of it) on this issue affect
   • recruiting procedures?
   • patterns of recruitment in traditionally male/female course areas?

Task 49 sets the context for thinking about equal opportunities in the college, but it is important to emphasize that in trying to provide equal opportunities it is necessary for course staff to be supported by college management. The FEU points out (in 'Women in post-16 education in Wales', 1989c) that equal opportunities can be effectively sustained in courses only when

• managers make appropriate executive decisions
• awareness-raising is supported by a consistent programme of change
• the raising of awareness affects not only all levels of staff in college but spreads out e.g. into schools, the careers service and even to elected members serving on LEA education committees and governing bodies
• the issue permeates in-house in-service training
• positive role-models can be used as exemplars
• students as well as staff are educated into equal opportunities.

At the level of the classroom and of teaching skills it is important for the tutor to consider what strategies will tend to eliminate prejudice when it creeps in and will promote positive attitudes. It is salutary to try to list some of these potential strategies. Table 27 attempts to do this, but leaves some gaps so that you can add your own ideas and lessons from experience.

It has to be admitted that there are some very difficult issues which cluster around this topic. Perhaps it is worthwhile to look at two extreme, but not unusual cases, and to realize that discrimination may operate against men as well as women.

1   All the students on an NNEB course are female. The course staff propose to recruit male students. News of this leaks into local infant schools and nursery units. There is an immediate and hostile reaction from parents who object to what they see as the dangers inherent in intimate care being given to small girls by male students.

TABLE 27   Teaching strategies to promote
awareness of equal opportunities for women

The successful teacher is likely . . .

- to be aware of the way he/she addresses individuals
- to be conscious of the hidden messages conveyed by classroom language
- to distribute tasks equitably, not by role stereotype
- to be conscious of his/her own attitudes
- to be aware of stereotypes in materials studied
- to be open to the discussion of equal opportunities' issues
- to be specially aware of the negative effects of visual images, e.g. in posters and visual aids
- to communicate (to employers and others involved with the course) the college policy
- to (actively) discourage unproductive 'battles of the sexes' in class
- to promote respect for all students and other staff on the basis of their personal worth.
-
-
-
-
-

2   All the students on a motor mechanics course are boys. For the coming year there are several applications from well-qualified girls. At a steering committee meeting this is reported to very supportive local employers. Initially they don't take the matter seriously, but later put up resistance. In addition, the college has a problem because the mechanical engineering block has only very low-quality male toilets and no changing facilities for girls.

Task 50   Responding to problems relating to equal opportunities

1   How would you respond to the problems outlined in the two short case-studies above?

2   The solutions to these problems are not simple. Suggest a long-term strategy for dealing with them.

3   Assume that male students are recruited to the NNEB course and female students to the mechanical engineering certificate. What would course staff then need to do to ensure that the newly recruited students receive equal treatment?

Equal opportunities: some multicultural issues

No-one can avoid gender issues when discussing the matter of equal opportunities. With multicultural issues the matter is more variable: some colleges will have a strong and varied racial mix, but in some there will be so few students from ethnic minority groups that it will be possible to retreat into an unacceptable position. In such a college one often hears the views expressed: 'We don't have a race problem, so we don't need in-service education on multicultural matters. There are no black students here.'

As with the gender issue, so with the multicultural one: much of the response to this problem is in raising awareness and then forging out appropriate policies and their resultant practices. Some interesting work has been done at the Central Manchester College, and reported in the FEU newsletter 'Anti-racist strategies in college and community' (1989d). One particularly useful section of this report concerns ways which tutors can vet curriculum materials for racism. This appears in our text as Table 28.

Experiments with ethnic monitoring have been going on for a number of years, notably in ILEA. An account of this can be found in Sammonds and Newbury 1989. From 1 September 1990 all colleges have collected ethnic monitoring data. The system works like this: colleges include a question on their enrolment form which asks for a response to a question about ethnic origin.

> The classification to be used in the FESR return is as follows:
> White
> Black – African
> Black – Caribbean
> Black – Other (please describe)
> Indian
> Pakistani
> Bangladeshi
> Chinese
> Any other ethnic group (please describe)
> Prefer not to say
> This is the modified classification developed by the Office of Population, Censuses and Surveys for the proposed question on ethnic group in the 1991 Census.
>
> People descended from more than one ethnic or racial group should be asked to complete their enrolment form on the basis of the group to which they consider they belong, or else to use the 'Any other ethnic group' category giving a description of their background.

TABLE 28   A checklist for anti-racist materials evaluation

1 Why did you choose to borrow this specific text?

2 Did you intend it as background reference or for actual use in a lesson?

3 Would any part of the text be culturally unacceptable to your students?

4 Does the text encourage students to value minority cultures?

5 Were you able to use the texts in the ways you had intended? If not, why not? Were the difficulties within the text?

6 Is the text clear in its objectives? Internally coherent? Sound in methodology?

7 Does the text in any way underestimate the intelligence/maturity/experience of your students?

8 Are the contexts relevant to the current experiences of your students?

9 Is the language authentic and relevant to your students?

10 Does the text contain information which helps your students to survive in existing social systems? Does it help them to challenge and change those systems?

11 Does the text in any way reinforce gender, race, nation or class stereotypes?

12 Does the text in any way challenge and positively seek to counter stereotyping?

13 Does it attempt to help students develop language skills for use in situations of racial discrimination/abuse?

14 Is the material attractively presented? (Quality of paper, print, illustrations, etc.)

15 Is there any part of the text that you would particularly recommend to other teachers?

16 Is there any part of the text to which you have particularly strong objections?

17 Would the text benefit particularly from being used in conjunction with other texts, possible bilingual texts? Please specify.

18 Do you know of similar but better texts that are not available in the Resource Centre and which you would recommend we acquired?

19 Would the text be suitable for independent student learning?

20 If the text is not suitable for your students, can you identify any students for whom it would be?

(Reproduced by permission of FEU

Data collection of itself, however, is of little value. As with gender, so with race: equal opportunities can flow only from situations in which awareness is raised, attitudes are changed and behaviour of tutor and students is appropriate. You should be aware of the excellent training pack RP390 available from FEU (2 Orange Street, London WC2H 7WE).

In many college courses there are opportunities to build on wide cultural experience among students and to incorporate these quite positively and deliberately into courses. The following are simply a few examples of interesting practice:

- ethnic traditions used to broaden experience in catering courses
- multicultural festival traditions built into NNEB/BTEC and other caring courses for communication to young children

- multicultural activities built into the social calendar of events in college, such as a 'Vietnamese Evening'
- work in courses such as art, photography and beauty therapy built around ethnic fashions and the treatment of different skin types
- religious beliefs other than Christianity considered as part of examination courses in Religious Education and non-examination general education courses.

▶ Task 51   Responding to multicultural issues in planning the curriculum

1   Some validating bodies require, others accept without the element of obligation, the inclusion of multicultural elements. Examine your own curriculum and the requirements of the validating bodies. Where and how could you become pro-active in building-in multicultural approaches in the courses for which you are responsible?
2   Encourage your colleagues to review the curriculum of these courses and contribute to appropriate emendations.
3   If necessary, negotiate these emendations with the validating bodies concerned, via the college committee structure where required.

The FEU recommends a series of steps which college managements can take to promote equal opportunities:

College management should:
- plan and develop a 'whole-college' approach to staff development for a multicultural society;
- initiate ethnic monitoring and needs analysis as part of the programme;
- build upon initiatives taken by committed staff members;
- monitor the day-to-day life of the college to identify staff development needs as they arise in incidents and events;
- review and improve procedures in staff selection to achieve representation of ethnic minorities;
- monitor and support departmental initiatives, meeting practical needs such as cover of classes of staff under training;
- recognize the crucial role of the principal, especially in mainly white colleges, in showing high visibility in pioneering staff development for a multicultural society;
- follow up on issues which come to light in staff development activities but require action in other management areas.

College management and academic boards should:

- scrutinize the environment and ethos of the college to uncover factors which might militate against multicultural interests and initiate staff development to change them;
- review the organizational structure of the college to identify needs for change to meet multicultural interests and support changes with staff development;
- ensure the continuous review of the curriculum to meet the needs of multicultural education and support curricular review with staff development activities such as staff–student working parties;
- review and improve procedures in student recruitment to ensure representation of ethnic minorities in the total student body and in distribution through the full range of courses;
- make multicultural consideration a standing item on agendas of all meetings concerned with the curriculum in its widest sense to ensure college staff development in this field. (FEU 1988b)

Equal opportunities: physical handicap

It is not only gender and racial issues that lend themselves to students feeling disadvantaged. Another very specific group which may find FE courses inhospitable are the physically handicapped. There are two kinds of barrier to integrating handicapped students into FE: attitudinal problems and physical problems. The attitudinal problems are to be resolved in ways not unlike those already discussed within this chapter, though tutors may like to follow up the specific theme by reading Dean and Heggarty (1984) or Segal (1984). Physical barriers, on the other hand, are very difficult for able-bodied people to understand. One particularly good piece of work by a social-care class was to simulate handicap (they blindfolded themselves, borrowed wheelchairs, etc.) and then try to carry on using the college site. You might care to project yourself into that situation in your own college.

Task 52   Simulating physical handicap

I   Imagine you have each of the following handicaps. In each case how well would you cope if you were a student trying to follow one of your own courses?
(a) You are confined to a wheelchair.
(b) You are blind.
(c) You are physically fit but profoundly deaf.
(d) You are deaf and dumb.

     (e) You are physically active but have to use callipers to get around.

     (f)   You are generally fit but have a colostomy.

2   What does this Task tell you about equal opportunities for handicapped students in your own college?

Equal opportunities: a summary

In looking at the issues related so far in this Unit there has been no attempt to deal in depth with each problem-area. The teaching skills required to deal with particular problems raised here have been dealt with in more or less detail as befits a manual of teaching skills for non-specialists in these fields. So, for example, no special skill may be needed to teach the active student who has a colostomy – though some understanding and facilities may be. But to teach the profoundly deaf may require specialist in-service training or specialist experience which is outside the scope of this Unit, such as training in sign language.

One issue not outside its scope, however, is that of the skill required to teach students with mild learning difficulties or similar special needs. Such students will be found in many FE courses. They suffer from a range of educational handicaps: poor numeracy, limited levels of reading ability, poor capacity to write, and so on. Often such students are directed to special-needs courses where specialist staff will teach them; but many access into craft courses, City and Guilds certificate courses, and onto other practical programmes in the FE sector. Indeed, more and more LEAs are defining policies which encourage less able youngsters to stay on into the FE sector to gain appropriate readiness for work.

Many such youngsters are taught for much of their college life by non-specialist staff; and, conversely, many FE tutors spend at least some of their working week trying to cater for such youngsters. Some basic advice for handling work with these slower learners is set out in Table 29.

TABLE 29   Handling slow learners in FE classes

It will be of assistance to the tutor . . .

- to assess all students' basic skills early on in the life of the course
- to identify those students who thereby emerge as having special learning needs
- in each case, to isolate the specific learning difficulty/ies involved
- to treat each special-needs student as an individual
- to avoid *public* identification of the student
- to plan out, as far as possible, individual patterns of work that will help these individuals
- when dealing with the whole class, to be aware of the language level of the less able, and the suitability of your language for those students

- in class, to pitch tasks so that they can be carried out at a variety of levels
- in class, to explain clearly what is required and repeat explanations and instructions
- to monitor these students and keep them under close, if unobtrusive, scrutiny
- to stimulate where possible through praise which is genuinely earned
- to replace written work by other media of communication if appropriate, e.g. sound or videotape, or use of a word-processor
- to use plenty of visual aids, models or other concrete examples
- to be patient
- to find ways of measuring and communicating progress to the student, however small the progression
- to give pastoral support where required
- to seek specialist advice on specific problems, e.g. dyslexia.

The last three Units have concentrated on particular groups of students. But the time has come to move on to a group of Units which deal with tutor skills, specifically with the administrative or managerial aspects of the tutor or course tutor's role.

Unit 14

COPING WITH ADMINISTRATIVE TASKS

Those of us who came into the teaching profession a while back had no inkling that the job of the teacher would develop into one with such a heavy load of administrative work. When the process began it was common enough to hear tutors say things like 'I didn't come into this job to be a secretary.' But now, most tutors accept that administration takes up a significant proportion of non-teaching time and does not attract secretarial assistance. Perhaps it would surprise many, even now, just how much time is spent in this way. Task 53 may help to clarify the matter for you.

▶ **Task 53 Assessing the quantity of administrative tasks in your role**

1   Keep a log of one week's work selected at random. (It would be useful to avoid the first and last week of a term as this may skew the result.)
2   A coding system of the kind shown in Table 30 will help you both save time in writing up the log *and* analyse the different kinds of administrative tasks you have to undertake.
3   To keep the log, use a proforma of the kind displayed in Table 30.
4   At the end of the week add up the total administrative time spent, and work this figure out as a percentage of total time.
5   Work out the proportion of total administrative time spent on each sub-task.

TABLE 30   A sample log for recording administrative tasks

	Administration	Teaching
Monday 0830	Corr	
0845	Ph	
0900		
0915		
0930		TI
0945		
1000		
1015	Mtg	
1030		
1045		
1100		
1115		T2
1130		
1145	Rec	
1200		
1215		
1230		
		Lunch

(and so on for the rest of Monday, and the remaining days of the week.)

Administration codes:	Teaching codes:
Corr – reading/writing letters	TI, T2 – teaching/tutorials
Rec – keeping student records/reports	P – preparation
Mtg – non-academic meetings	CD – curriculum development
Ph – phone calls made/received	CC – curriculum committees/working groups

What you have discovered now is how much time you spend on administrative activities. This will highlight some important issues, such as:

- How efficiently do you use your time?
- How organized are you?
- Can you prioritize tasks effectively?
- Do you plan ahead, or let administrative tasks creep up on you?
- Do you have the necessary skills to work efficiently at your administration?

The Oxford Dictionary defines administration as: 'the management of public or business affairs . . . the people who administer an organisation . . . '. It defines an administrator as: 'a person responsible for administration; one who has a talent for this . . . ' (Oxford Dictionary, 1990). You may feel the latter part of this definition is certainly open to question, when, as a tutor, you are required to carry out numerous administrative tasks, often without secretarial assistance. Therefore, with a 'talent for this' or not, it is part of the job! Teaching in Further Education usually requires great skills of management and organization, not least of *your time*.

The year-plan

Many offices in commercial and business premises carry a year-planner. To buy and display data on a commercial year-planner (and they are available in academic-year versions) is not strictly necessary, although it may be quite a practical thing to do and it promotes a feeling of professional competence. Whether using this kind of aid or not, a year-plan is important.

Task 54   Completing a year-plan

First of all, plot all the administrative tasks relating to your courses onto your planner at the appropriate time of the year. Include prospective and present students in your planning by detailing the time of year to:

- start advertizing your courses
- hold open evenings
- visit local high schools
- interview prospective students
- offer places
- arrange work placements
- mark course work
- mark examination papers
- complete Records of Achievement
- write references.

Add to this list all the other administrative tasks you undertake on a regular cycle, to complete your plan for the year.

The term-plan

Your year-plan will probably have shown how some terms or parts of terms make more administrative demands on your time than others. If you realize this from the start of the autumn term, you can ensure that a greater amount of lesson planning and assignment planning is done at the most convenient time. This insight itself leads to the important observation that administration should not be seen as separate from other organization and planning, e.g. academic. When planning for individual terms you need to consider these other aspects of planning; that is, consider each course individually. For each one, plan your lesson content and associated assignments, so that you are aware of the preparation necessary. Thus, for each course you may divide the curriculum up into weekly blocks, with an indication of when assignments fall and what they will assess:

Week	Curriculum	Assessment
1	The camera: how it works	
2	Developing film	Informal – via feedback from
3	Processing prints	student results
4	Composition	
5	Lighting	
6	Creating effects	Set up formal assignment
7	Assignment: Project work	
8	on a theme	Formal – course work
9		Display used as critique and
10	Display of work	feedback to individuals.

Ensure that 'deadlines' for assignments are entered as they will require time set aside for marking. Guest speakers may also be required which will require substantial time to arrange, so plan to spend time on this and the arrangement of student visits if required by particular subject areas (e.g. visits to religious centres).

Meetings and the necessary paperwork they entail also need to be planned well in advance, and most Further Education tutors will have schedules equally as demanding as your own. Therefore you need to set out at the beginning of each term to arrange the meetings for which you are responsible at well-spaced intervals. This will provide you with adequate time to prepare and collate information to present at the meetings, and time following this to disseminate further information and minutes of the meetings to your colleagues.

The weekly/daily diary

The diary has a respectable history. Pepys used it to record the minutiae of daily life; minutiae that turned into significant social history as well as a poignant autobiography. In the Victorian era pale ladies wrote precious thoughts in the privacy of their boudoirs and on locked pages. Today we probably think most readily of Del Boy's Filofax and regard the diary as an object of mild pretention. Forget all these images. Think of the diary as a tool and use it; for example, to:

- keep records of appointments
- keep your department secretary informed of your whereabouts by keeping a copy
- plan placement visiting
- plan tasks ahead and remind yourself to do them
- record jobs completed
- preserve 'key thoughts' for later action
- keep records, e.g. of journeys made, expenses to be claimed
- provide data on your workload and its patterns for future planning
- note down dates of e.g. festivals celebrated by a range of ethnic groups: Yom Kippur, Divali, Chinese New Year.

Some additional aids to efficiency

In this Unit so far we have looked at the planning aspect of coping with administrative and organizational tasks – at recording annual, weekly or daily events and using the records to promote efficiency. Next we make three general suggestions about improving administrative efficiency.

1 Evolve a system
What we mean by this is that a regular work-pattern will help to improve your efficiency and save time. It is almost certain that those who deal with administrative tasks in a disciplined, routine way deal with them best. So a period *before* the working day (if you are a 'lark') or *after* it (if you are an 'owl') will keep you up to date. By contrast, treat with suspicion those who put aside a weekly slot (these days life moves on too quickly for this, and weekly attention to tasks will mean deadlines are by then too close or even passed). The tutor who once said, with genuine pride, 'I save all my paperwork up till the end of term' was not only inefficient but irresponsible and unprofessional. Colleagues had to carry that workload and protect themselves and the students from the appalling consequences of that cynical policy.

2 Filing
If 'time is of the essence' then you need to lay your hands on information quickly. This requires a simple, but effective, *filing system*. Each course will require a *separate file* containing sections. You need to retain *all* course information, as it may be needed in the future and time will be saved by storing it carefully: e.g., standard letters requesting work placements for students should be retained for the following term.

3   *The instant index*

Another time-saving aid is an *index* of contacts to include names, addresses, telephone numbers and special curriculum-area for future reference e.g. 'Mary Nelson . . . multi-cultural issues/working with children and their families.'

People are the most valuable resource in education, therefore an index of tutors and guest speakers with particular strengths is a vital asset to your administrative system and, subsequently, your course.

Written communication

One of the key skills in administration is the course-communication. This can be of various kinds: papers for working groups, agendas, internal memos and so on. But in this section we shall concentrate on written communication with the outside world, something which is too frequently neglected but which is important for your own and the college's professional image.

Telephone conversations are quicker and often more convenient during a busy day, but a letter provides so much more in terms of:

- making and confirming arrangements or providing a reminder
- providing detailed information which can be read and re-read
- establishing a formal record
- providing a permanent record
- giving exactly the same message to a number of people if necessary.

It is worth developing the skill of good letter-writing for effective communication and quality service. *Remember* – every letter you send out represents the college. You are responsible for its reputation. Therefore, there are a few basic principles you need to learn and apply to your letter-writing, before you consider style and image; a good impression will be created by a well-structured letter. This may seem elementary, but one sees so many scrappy and illiterate examples that the points are worth rehearsing.

Planning a letter

You need to decide *what* you want to say, and *how* you are going to say it. Planning your letters will help you get them right the first time.

- First, decide on the reason for your letter – what do you want to achieve?
- Consider the recipient – what does he/she need to know?
- Make sure you have all the necessary information ready to assist you – including previous letters and any facts required.

- List everything you wish to include.
- Now arrange the points logically in order.

Structure

Layout is your next consideration. Your letter needs to be well structured to be easily read and understood. Always:

- start a new paragraph for each new point
- try to vary the length of each paragraph
- attempt to vary the length of each sentence
- try to keep sentences reasonably short
- try to keep words short – dated 'business words' are unacceptable in today's world – and always avoid jargon.

Headings

These can be useful for immediate recognition, i.e. the reason for the letter and the provenance will be apparent, for example:

Date:

Dear Sir/Madam

BTEC National Diploma in Health Studies:
Hospital Placements

Headings can help by making the letter shorter, because you must not repeat the heading in the opening paragraph. If you are replying to a letter with a heading, you can use the same one. Headings can also make filing easier for the recipient, especially if it is one of a series of letters.

Opening the letter

How to address the recipient depends on previous knowledge. If you know the recipient's name, always use it, e.g. 'Dear Mrs Banks'. Otherwise begin with 'Dear Sir/Madam'.

The first paragraph

Introduce the subject of your letter immediately if you have not used a heading. If you are replying to a letter, always acknowledge receipt of it at the beginning.

Following paragraphs

These should be in a logical order, clear and easy to read, giving or requesting information carefully.

The final paragraph

First and last impressions are important. You need to end your letter in a precise way which expresses your future expectations or intentions in a positive tone.

Closing the letter

If you have used the addressee's name, end with 'Yours sincerely'; if you have used Sir/Madam, end with 'Yours faithfully'. This is not an option, it is a *rule*. Following your own signature, it is a good idea to have your full name and title typed for information and identification.

Punctuation

Punctuation is important because it helps the recipient read and understand the letter more easily. Below is an aide-memoire of 'do's' and 'don'ts' in the use of punctuation marks.

	Do	Don't
Comma	Use a comma to indicate pauses. Use a comma to emphasize certain words. Use a comma to separate items in a list or series.	Use a comma instead of a full stop or a semi-colon between two separate sentences.
Full stop	Use a full stop to mark the end of a sentence.	Use a full stop at the end of a question. A question mark should always be used in this instance.
Colon	Use a colon to precede a summary, list or quotation.	
Semi-colon	Use a semi-colon to separate two parts of a long sentence.	Use a semi-colon where a colon is correct (see above).

Apostrophe	Use an apostrophe to indicate possession.	Use an apostrophe when 'its' refers to possession. Otherwise the word will mean an abbreviation of 'it is'.

Capital letters

These are often misused. Here is a list of their uses, for reference when writing letters:

- for days of the week
- for months of the year
- for proper nouns and titles, e.g. people's names, place names, books
- for times of the year, e.g. festivals of Christmas, Easter, Ramadan, Chinese New Year, Passover
- at the beginning of each sentence.

General points to remember

- Address letters to people by name and title. If you don't know these, try to find out!
- Where appropriate, keep letters relatively informal by use of 'I', e.g. 'I would like to thank you for your support of Rachel Johnson during her work placement.'
- Remember to include your telephone number *and extension number* in your letter for easier contact. Also, these days, include your fax number if you have one.

The aim of your correspondence is to project a professional yet caring image as a Further Education teacher. The way to achieve this is to plan your letters carefully as above, but allow your own personal flair to shine through. Remember, you represent the college, but also yourself, to your clients and prospective students.

It is important, too, to consider turnaround times. Correspondence should, ideally, be *answered* within one or two days at most. Longer delays convey a sloppy image. Letters which you generate should, of course, give plenty of notice (not just a day or two) of any deadlines contained in them.

It is inevitable that some letters and communications will be photocopies. Remember to allow for printing-time when setting deadlines in photocopied communications. But remember, too, to consider carefully the issue of a personal signature. It really is worth spending three minutes signing twenty letters personally if the ultimate result is client goodwill!

Task 55   Examining correspondence

Consider the letter which follows and note the professional, yet personal, style of communication. What messages does the letter convey? Does the letter reflect *your* image as a course tutor? If not, decide what changes you would make to the letter to reflect your personality, style of communication and corporate 'college' policy.

Date:

Dear ....

I am writing to you at the beginning of the summer break so that you can relax after your examinations knowing that a place has been reserved for you on one of the following courses:

BTEC First Diploma in Health and Care Studies
BTEC National Diploma in Caring Services (Nursery Nursing).

Your exam results will determine which course you take up, as we discussed at your interview. Once you receive your results, complete the enclosed form and return it to me to arrive no later than 1st September, 1991.

You need to write to the Local Education Office in High Street for a set of grant forms as soon as possible. One of the forms – FEA/4 – needs to be stamped by the college, so send this to me when it arrives. If you need any help at all with any of the forms, don't hesitate to contact me for assistance.

Your work placements will take up one day per week and you will need to wear an overall, details of which are enclosed. The firm concerned needs to have all orders by 12th August, 1991.

Enrolment day is *Tuesday 3rd September, 1991*. Please come to *Room M14 at 2.00 p.m.* If you cannot enrol on that day, let me know in writing.

Your name and address have been sent to the Medical Officer of Health. You will be asked to attend a medical at your local medical centre, or at college, and will be given an appointment time. It is very important that you keep the appointment. If it is not possible for you to attend, then telephone for another date to be made.

I hope you enjoy your summer holiday and I look forward to meeting you again in September.

Yours sincerely,

Jane Smith
Tutor for BTEC Care

Using the telephone

Finally in this Unit we pause to consider the use of the telephone.

To sustain the professional image of the course, try to ensure that everyone who *answers* the telephone for the section:

- gives a brief, informative statement; e.g. 'This is the Horticulture Section, Jane Drummond speaking. How can I help you?'
- sounds welcoming
- is knowledgeable about colleagues and their whereabouts. (Wall-mounted timetables and office diaries help. Don't just say: 'He's not in today' – the client will always assume he's AWOL and off to the races!)
- is prepared to take a message.

In using the telephone, bear these factors in mind:

- Will it be more efficient than a letter?
- Are you prepared in what you want to say? Do you sound efficient?
- Have you remembered the courtesies of greeting and parting?

To conclude, a provocative thought perhaps:

When my fax learns to talk to your answerphone, will you and I be free, or just superfluous?

Unit 15

EXERCISING FINANCIAL CONTROL

Controlling a budget

In education in the 1990s the exercise of financial control has become a daily reality not just for principals and senior managers but also for many course staff. This Unit does not concern itself with the macro-level of college or faculty/department finance, but tries to look at issues arising from financial management at the course level. Nevertheless, some important general principles are discussed which apply equally in any college financial context.

Many tutors cut their financial teeth on a budget of hundreds of pounds, or a thousand or two intended for use with a single course; but even some individual course budgets are much higher than this. To handle this money efficiently and effectively the tutor will need to look at some key questions:

- How much have I got?
- How long has it got to last? (Usually the *financial* year)
- How many students/staff has it to provide for?
- What is legitimate expenditure within the college procedures?
- What is the correct college system for ordering goods?
- Is there a policy on where goods may be purchased?
- Can I take advantage of any educational discount systems?
- Are there any things I *must* purchase with the money (e.g. commitments to maintenance contracts)?
- Which other course staff should I consult about their students'/their needs?

- Which administrative officer in the college can help me with procedural queries?
- Should I set aside part of the sum as a contingency fund?
- Since all invoices should be paid within the financial year, what delivery times should I allow and what are the official closing dates for presenting invoices?
- Can I keep money over from one financial year to another?

Questions like those listed – and you may want to formulate some of your own to match your specific circumstances – will clear much of the ground for thinking about a budget. But while many people regard spending money as reasonably straightforward, controlling it can be a nerve-wracking issue for some. However, as is often the case, simple systems are often best. A common error is to say to oneself that financial purchases are the field of professional judgement, but financial control is best left to the college's financial officer. Experience suggests that this macro-system is *not* helpful for the proper control of a small devolved budget which is unquestionably more efficient when carried out by the nominated budget-holder, i.e. the tutor. To control the budget effectively all that is really needed is a notebook and a recording system for the following data:

- a note of the sum available in total
- known and planned commitments (costed as accurately as possible)
- invoices paid.

Of course, for those who control larger sums or who prefer other ways of working, all this can be put onto a computer spreadsheet. However, whether a manual or computerized system is used, the budget out-turn will be as accurate, or inaccurate, as the data fed into that system. A missed invoice, or failure to do commitment accounting, will lead to overspending; while accuracy and forward planning will avoid embarrassing errors!

Financial control is viewed by many with a degree of terror; but the preceding paragraphs have suggested that much fear is unfounded, subject to a few simple and methodical practices. Armed with these starting-points tutors can organize budgets at course level with extreme accuracy and efficiency.

 ## Task 56   Assessing your own budget situation

1   For any budgets which you hold, use the questions listed on page 131 to take stock of your own familiarity with the college's budget and financial control systems.

2   Review your manual or computerized financial control systems. Do they serve your needs adequately? Do they give you the knowledge you need to have when you need it?

Planning ahead and making professional judgements

Budget-holders do not simply have the responsibility for understanding the relevant financial systems and for keeping track of expenditure. It might even be argued that these parts of the process of budgeting are the *least* important. An effective budget-holder will do more than be efficient in these ways: he or she will make sure that budget planning becomes integral to all planning within the course. So the budget will help to shape the curriculum and the curriculum will determine the directions of spending within the budget. This last statement is a far-reaching one, and is worthy of amplification.

A course – any course – has to be taught within constraints. Non-financial constraints include, for example, the quality of the student intake, the number of available course hours, the strengths of the course staff, and so on. Obviously, the more able and motivated the students, the longer they are taught and the greater the strengths of the staff team, then arguably the better will be the course results. However, in practice there are always constraints on these factors so that the 'theoretical threshold of course effectiveness' is always unlikely to be achieved.

In the same way, financial issues can affect course effectiveness. A diploma course in the college of agriculture and horticultural studies has been favoured by access to the following resources:

- work experience in an ultra-modern on-site dairy unit
- three day-visits a year to dairy units around the country
- five speakers a year on issues related to dairy farming
- visit to an equipment manufacturing company
- access to the latest books and periodicals in the course collection
- a residential week in France to compare British and French dairy practice.

In the current financial year the course leader has been told he must cut the course budget by ten per cent. The task is then to decide which items to cut to save the appropriate sum, while retaining quality at its highest possible level. In these circumstances the course leader is likely to have to address the following questions:

- What, if any, of the resources listed above could be cut *completely* while doing minimal damage to course effectiveness?

- What, if any, of the resources could be bought *more cheaply* while being retained?
- What, if any, of the resources could be *curtailed* to provide a good service to students but at less cost?
- What alternative resources could be *substituted* for some of those listed; alternatives which could be less costly?

The course leader will, of course, have to make hard decisions. He may even have to resist a lot of pressure from course staff who have particular interests and motivations for sustaining certain activities. It is possible that a final set of decisions would look like those in Table 31; and the reasons for those decisions would need to be articulated, too, as is summarized in the right-hand column of Table 31.

It will be seen from the example quoted that financial constraints affect course content and the way courses are delivered, i.e. the curriculum. So, financial planning and curriculum planning do indeed need to go hand in hand, as was suggested above. Conversely, changes to the curriculum (either content, delivery, or both) of any given course do affect financial matters. So a decision to introduce a new element in a syllabus in place of an existing one has implications regarding textbooks, library resources and so on. Planning for a course has to be all of a piece, and tutors cannot logically claim that curriculum issues are in the professional domain but financial ones are not.

A course leader must also face another important issue that is bound to surface sooner or later: the view of some staff that any curriculum problem is soluble if the college management throws enough money at it! While there *is* an element of truth in the position that improved facilities can improve course effectiveness (that is, the performance of students), money remains only one – and probably not the most significant – factor in the equation. We have seen in the example quoted above that real savings can be achieved, alternative strategies sought, and even cuts made while preserving the essential integrity of a course. One sometimes comes across a course leader or tutor whose stock reaction to any new direction or request for accountability for course quality is countered by: 'We need more resources.' While *sometimes* this may be true, often the response needs amending to 'We need more resourcefulness.' In one case known to us, a course leader whose initial response was always as described complained to the line manager that the course was underprivileged and under-resourced. Upon investigation of the year's orders, it was discovered that all the course budget had been spent, all invoices paid, but there was no trace of any of the goods – the students were indeed struggling with no equipment. Later, it emerged that all the ordered items had been taken to, and stockpiled on, another site. The budget officer had signed the invoices but not checked that the goods had been received! Experience suggests that complaints about lack of financial resources are always worth careful scrutiny by the course leader.

TABLE 31   Making a ten per cent cut in a course budget: strategies and reasons

Budget activity	Action	Reasons for action
1 Sustaining a modern dairy unit	Facility retained in full	Fundamental to course/work experience. To keep up-to-date any expenditure would be small relative to the course budget, so savings negligible.
2 Visits to British dairy units	Cut to two; those close at hand	Main costs are travel and subsistence; by cutting to two half-day visits, carefully chosen, little learning is lost, but a modest sum is saved.
3 Five visiting speakers	Programme sustained; speakers changed	To date, speakers have been working farmers paid a consultancy fee. Now the invited speakers will be from public bodies – MPs etc. – who will not require fees. Some change of emphasis, but still a good programme. Significant savings.
4 Visit to equipment manufacturer	Cut completely	Lecture programme amended to fill in for some loss. Good saving.
5 Latest books and periodicals	Careful pruning; new purchasing systems	All the best periodicals retained; some periodicals jettisoned, and book material vetted. Buy books via bookseller, not direct, and negotiate rates. Small loss of facility; small savings.
6 Residential	Cutback in time and level of provision	Programme cut to basics – visit reduced to three days. A small loss of learning and some loss of social benefits. Off-peak travelling times reduces travel cost. Hotel changed. Some marginal loss of learning. Significant savings.

► ## Task 57   Getting best value from your own course budget

1   Apply the questions listed earlier in this section to any budgets for which you are responsible:
- Could any resources be *cut completely* while doing minimal damage to the course?
- What resources could be *bought more cheaply*?
- What could be *curtailed*, so providing a good service to students at less cost?
- What alternative resources could be *substituted* to provide the same service at less cost?

2   If you are not in a cost-cutting situation with your budget(s), the exercise above may still have cut costs. How could any savings made through this exercise be best utilized?

Looking at the context of course budgets

In this Unit we have given some attention to the skills of financial management likely to be required of a tutor/course leader, and we have seen how these and the curriculum of a course are interrelated. The last section of this Unit is designed to provide some general information about contexts in which course budgets in colleges exist, so that this broader perspective can inform the thinking of tutors and course leaders. Those who aspire to become heads of departments or faculties would need to address the issues here in greater depth by consulting the bibliography.

First, a course budget is only part of a department/faculty budget, and that wider perspective is important. At the department/faculty level, the head will have to look not only at supplies and services costs but at staffing costs. At this level, decisions will be made about the number of full-time equivalent (FTE) staff who can be allotted to teach the course. This decision will depend upon a number of factors such as the financial position of the department/faculty and the minimum validation requirements of the course. Once that decision is made it will have a number of significant effects on the course leader's planning of:

- the number and range of staff available
- the number of hours students can be taught
- the quantity of tutorial time available
- the level of work-placement supervision.

All these, and other resulting issues, will have an effect on the curriculum and delivery of an individual course.

Another concern at department/faculty level may be the generation of income through full-cost courses. Many colleges are now becoming conscious of their ability to sell expertise, especially in the form of courses or consultancies. The generation of income in one area of operation may help the basic level of resources in another. At the level of the individual course, however, there may also be penalties: for example, able staff may have part of their teaching hours diverted from a course which is not too income-generating to one which is.

At college level, too, these and similar financial considerations will have effects that filter down to the individual course level. One contentious issue in many colleges is the 'differential' treatment of students from one department/faculty to another. Consider, for example, the data in Table 32.

TABLE 32   Cost per full-time equivalent student of courses in Hotstuff College, broken down by department (excluding staff costs)

Department	£ per FTE student
Electrical and electronic engineering	£127.34
Art and design	£110.51
Mechanical engineering	£ 99.27
Horticultural studies	£ 83.60
Management studies	£ 75.24
Business studies	£ 68.80
Science	£ 67.93
Humanities	£ 42.27
Law	£ 38.55
Social studies	£ 26.11
General studies	£ 19.01

The costs in Table 32 appear to indicate that electrical and electronic engineering students are treated more favourably than general studies students. But this 'differential' may be an illusion: the engineering students will need expensive equipment with which to work, while general studies students may simply need access to some educational visits and some quite basic classroom resources (textbooks etc.) in order to achieve equivalent successful results. Table 32 may well mask real financial issues that a college would need to explore (for example, is humanities work really 61.9 per cent more expensive to do successfully than social studies?). But, from the point of view of a tutor/course leader it is important to understand that the apparent differentials are necessary even if one might wish to dispute matters of detail and investigate the financial efficiencies of each department.

Obviously, too, at college level all sorts of broader financial issues have to be addressed, which will not be the direct concern of the tutor/course leader but which eventually act as a constraint on the budget available to him or her. These broad issues include premises costs, the costs of administrative support, global staffing costs, costs of transporting students where applicable, infrastructure costs (e.g. canteen), and so on. The message here is that the individual tutor can no longer afford to write off these processes as irrelevant or as the concern of others: all of us have to work within the resulting constraints and would therefore do well to understand them.

The financial management of courses is an important aspect of management skills in the education world of the 1990s, and tutors now have to expect to be actively involved in some level of financial management. Everyone involved in a course – staff and students – depends on the good management of the course leader in financial issues as well as the more traditional academic and pastoral ones. This Unit has suggested that a reasonable level of both competence and understanding is within the reach of every tutor.

Unit 16

DEALING WITH OUTSIDE AGENCIES

The range of outside agencies

Back in the 1960s sociometry was a popular way to study the dynamics of classrooms. Some students became 'sociometric stars'; that is, they were the ones (in contrast to 'isolates') who drew to themselves the majority of social interactions and were most frequently chosen as friends or work-partners. Since most Further Education tutors, certainly those who take on course responsibilities, are also the centre of interactions, they too become a kind of 'sociometric star'. This is shown diagrammatically in Figure 3.

In this Unit we look at just five *main* kinds of agency beyond college with which course tutors and leaders are likely to have dealings. These, and their 'agents' are:

- *Professional support agencies* – these usually take the form of national or regional groups of tutors who teach similar ranges of courses to one another. In practical terms, regional groups provide front-line support to tutors on a local level.

- *Teaching agencies* – by this we mean contributors to courses who are 'beyond college'; usually visiting speakers. They may be local employers who are asked to give students insights into the world of work,

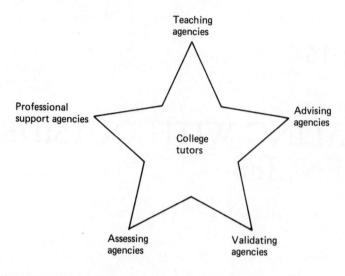

Figure 3   Links with outside agencies

other practitioners with relevant specialist knowledge (e.g. health visitors,
artists), or eminent teachers from other
colleges or private consultancies.

- *Validating agencies*   – almost all courses are now subject to
some form of external validation. The
processes to achieve this often involve
prolonged contacts with Boards, some
of it in person, some on paper. Often
there are validating visits, where college
and course provision are scrutinized by
representatives from the Board. This is
now a key task for course staff at all
levels in Further and Higher education.

- *Assessing agencies*   – once validated, there are ongoing contacts to be sustained with agents
variously called assessors, moderators
or examiners.

- *Advising agencies*   – these are many, and range from consultants used voluntarily by the college to
look at specific issues, through HMI,
LEA advisers or inspectors, advisory
teachers/lecturers, TVEI and TEED personnel and even auditors (though we

shall not be talking about this last group here, since they are more likely to deal initially with senior or middle managers).

As a backdrop to looking at the roles of outside agencies and their representatives it is important to remember that relationships are two-way processes. Both sides have information necessary, or useful, for the other – it is a reciprocal relationship between professionals. With this in mind, this Unit will now look at each of the agencies in turn.

Professional support agencies

These are very much agencies with which, as professionals, we *choose* to deal. They provide outlets in which to meet colleagues informally, gain insights and participate in course-related activity with like-minded others. As teachers, we find out a great deal by sharing information with our colleagues; and due to the amount of stress associated with our job, colleagues often provide much-needed support.

Colleagues from other colleges often understand the particular pressures of courses they run in common with others, which is why 'associations' have sprung up which are formed by teachers of particular subjects/courses. They are usually regional in nature and meet half-termly, termly or annually. The information shared can be quite valuable, particularly to new members of staff. Individual needs can be catered for in terms of the membership itself suggesting agendas for subsequent meetings. This way, the needs of the group and individual members are met, and staff development is really the key to their success. Information provided at these association meetings can concern:

- course format
- course mode – full-time/part-time
- course content
- integration of subjects
- use of resources
- entry requirements
- course administration
- types of work placement and modes of placement – e.g. block placement/one day per week
- types of assignment
- teaching and learning strategies.

The list is endless. Obviously a great deal can be gained from listening to each others' successes and failures, initiatives and experiments. Time and effort can be saved by this mode of secondhand experiential learning.

Finally on this topic, let it be said that the tutor who gains in experience may wish in turn to become an officer of the regional association. These groups do not run themselves and often depend on loyal and hardworking volunteers. It could be to both the college's and your own advantage to consider a more active role in your local association as you gain confidence.

Teaching agencies

Most courses are privileged, from time to time, to have the wisdom and increased perspective that can be gained through the use of outside speakers. But, as a tutor, you will need to understand how to organize such events to best advantage.

If you were inviting a visiting speaker or specialist teacher to talk to a group of students you would probably make your first contact by telephone, followed by a confirmation in writing. Your letter would need to contain information about:

- name of course and number of students
- theme of talk(s)
- date(s)
- time(s)
- venue – site, building and room
- resources available
- rate of pay
- a reply slip, which would need to be attached for information concerning requests for OHP/video and confirmation of the intent to teach on that particular occasion(s).

In addition to this, you would also need to enclose a copy of:

- the timetable for the course – giving titles of sessions (subject areas) and associated personnel with the addressee's session highlighted
- the syllabus for that unit of the course/subject area with the addressee's contribution highlighted.

These two enclosures are essential, as the speaker needs to know where he/she fits into the rest of the course and the overall aims of the course.

Validating agencies

In Unit 4 we looked at the detailed process of compiling a course document; that is, how to compile a curriculum proposal and then document it in a form suitable either for use in-house or for external validation purposes. This section assumes that you have been through that process and deals only with the administrative contacts which you are likely to have in order to get a course validated by an external agency subsequent to its approval through your own college systems. The degree to which course tutors (as opposed to middle or senior managers) have direct involvement in this process is variable from institution to institution – though the task falls increasingly on section or course leaders.

Assessing agencies

The main consideration here is the *type* of information to pass on to the assessor. Different assessors will require different information, and their role may overlap with the advisory role when necessary (see below). The following paragraphs try to give an indication of some of the information an assessor may require:

- *Aims, objectives and rationale of the course/unit/subject area*
  The assessor needs to know the purpose of your course and where it is leading the students. This is particularly important for an NVQ assessed course, as the NVQ assessor may be looking for specific vocational elements. (See details later in this Unit.)
- *Course/subject area/unit content*
  The assessor will need to know specific details of indicative content to assess relevance, breadth of learning and range of skills to be developed.
- *Work placements*
  The type and range of placement will be considered in terms of relevance and mode of attendance. You will need to provide the reasoning to support your selection of one day per week/block placements. Assessment of students whilst on placement will also be looked at with regard to placement report forms completed by placement personnel.
- *Teaching and learning strategies*
  A variety of styles appropriate to the course will be looked for by the assessors.
- *Assignments/course work/examinations*
  Continuous assessment and examinations are a focal point of the assessors' role. They are concerned with not only *what* is assessed but *how* it is assessed.
- *Weighting*
  Weighting of assignments or examination marks as parts of the whole is important to the assessors. It establishes the importance of particular

pieces of work or exams to the complete qualification awarded at the end of the course.
- *Integration*
  This is another vital element of course design favoured by assessors, due to the fact that it proves that the students are understanding and applying the knowledge and skills they have learnt on the course across subject areas.

This is particularly important for national vocational qualifications. NVQ assessors look in terms of outcomes, that is, what must be achieved rather than the process of learning.

The National Council requires each NVQ to be divided into units of competence. Each unit relates to competence in a different area of activity within a job. Each unit will consist of elements of skill, knowledge and understanding and specify the performance required to demonstrate competence.

Criteria used in assessment

Assessors will also be keen to look at the criteria used when course work/ exams are marked. They usually expect a detailed breakdown of points looked for by markers. In the case of course work, they usually expect the students to be given a good idea of what is expected to reach particular marks, e.g.:

85% + – *Distinction*	Very high skill level; shows originality and ability to develop own ideas and skills.
65–84% – *Merit*	Considerable command of skill and shows capability and potential.
45–64% – *Pass*	Sound skill level. Average orthodox work.
30–44% – *Referral*	Limited skill level and can only manage with considerable help and support.
less than 30% – *Fail*	Fails to reach basic skill level.

Common/transferable skills

When common skills are graded, assessors usually like to see the skills themselves broken down into smaller areas, e.g. *common skills – practical skills.*

Scientific and creative skills, for example, could be separated into the following categories: the student should

1   demonstrate the ability to work safely in the workplace
2   select, use and where relevant maintain processes, materials, tools and equipment suitable for the purpose
3   demonstrate competence in investigative skills and scientific method
4   demonstrate ability in a wide range of manipulative skills
5   prepare and implement designs using such skills
6   identify and review the application of scientific and technological development within the workplace
7   undertake individual and/or group project(s) relevant to own vocational area involving practical/creative skills.

Task 58   Examining common/transferable skills

Take each of the transferable skills you have identified for your own students' development and break each one down into separate categories in a similar way.

Advising agencies

As indicated earlier in this Unit, these are increasing in number – especially as initiatives like TVEI and the establishment of government agencies like Training Enterprise and Education Department come onstream. In this Unit the most useful things we can do to help tutors are, perhaps, to draw together some common threads in answer to the question:

'What do advisers or inspectors look for?'

In Table 33 we have attempted to draw up a checklist of generic items that are commonly explored by advisory bodies. All these 'advisers' do, of course, have a monitoring role; all of them look for quality in one aspect or another (so it may be worthwhile to refresh your memory about Unit 10). The checklist in Table 33 is generic – it does not, nor could it, show all the nuances that any particular adviser from a specific advisory body might look for.

Before examining the Table you might like to reflect on the purpose of this kind of quality control. Basically, what we are dealing with here is quality assurance: satisfying the external agent that the course is meeting its *declared intentions* for students in an *effective manner*. (Both are important: good examination results can be achieved despite poor teaching, but the *process* of education has an importance alongside the outcomes.) If you, as the professional, adopt an attitude to courses which is quality-conscious and scrutinizes your own and your students' activities objectively and systematically to eradicate problems (the process of total quality management or TQM), then you may have things to learn from advice and monitoring, but it should not be a process which is fear-inducing or stress-laden. In the dim past, monitoring was very judgemental. Those days have gone, and there is much more sharing now; sharing of collective wisdom by fellow professionals towards mutually agreed objectives.

Task 59   Examining the quality of your own course

Before completing this Unit, go over the items in Table 33. Try to prepare yourself for a real or imaginary visit by an adviser – from HMI, the LEA or TVEI for example – by preparing what you would say about your course against each heading.

Finally, when you have completed Task 59, you will be more confident about carrying out the work in Unit 17, which looks at promoting your course to potential clients and students.

TABLE 33 Aspects of courses which are commonly explored by advisers and inspectors

1   The nature of the course:
   - course documentation
   - the intentions and objectives of the course
   - numbers on roll
   - current drop-out rate and reasons for drop-out
   - validating body
   - date of re-validation
   - staffing arrangements
   - qualifications of staff and their appropriateness
   - financial resource issues
   - accommodation and its suitability
   - timetables and annual programmes, e.g. of work experience
   - place of the course in the department/faculty portfolio
   - progression routes

2   Course content:
   - relevance to course intentions
   - suitability to the student group
   - breadth
   - balance
   - interrelationships (e.g. between theory and practice)
   - up-to-dateness

3   Teaching and learning methods:
    * variety of teaching methods
    * use of audio-visual presentation, information technology, etc.
    * opportunities for self-study
    * library and information technology support systems
    * amount and quality of hands-on experience for students
    * variety of learning strategies, e.g. problem-solving, projects
    * evidence of planned professional development and up-dating of staff

4   Tutorial and other support:
    * arrangements for one-to-one support
    * arrangements for group tutorials
    * quality of student–student relations
    * quality of staff–student relations
    * careers advice and information

5   Work-experience arrangements:
    * location and timing of work-experience placements
    * processes for obtaining and vetting placement locations
    * relations with placement providers
    * arrangements for tutors' supervision of placements
    * joint provider–tutor assessment procedures

6   Assessment arrangements
    * nature and timing of assessments
    * variety and appropriateness of assessment methods
    * nature and effectiveness of feedback to students
    * balance of practical and theoretical assessments
    * methods and effectiveness of recording achievements of students

7   Relations with the relevant employment sector:
    * nature of formal links, e.g. via course committee
    * nature of informal links
    * staff updating in work situations
    * awareness by staff of changing workplace practices
    * use of employment-sector staff in assessing and delivering aspects of the course

8   The management of the course:
    * effectiveness and efficiency of course administration
    * effectiveness and efficiency of personnel (staff) management
    * effectiveness and efficiency of financial management
    * course manager's liaison with outside agencies
    * course quality-control systems
    * course manager's college/regional/national perspectives

9   Performance indicator data:
    * numbers of students enrolled (over three- to five-year period)
    * staff–student ratios
    * students' drop-out rate for this period (with reasons)

- examination pass rates for the period
- students' employment destinations for the period
- students' progressing to further training for the period
- data relating to access, e.g. in respect of race, gender
- opinions of students about the course
- how student opinion is collected and used by course staff
- opinions of other 'stakeholders', e.g. potential employers
- the extent to which 'performance targets' are set by course staff
- the means by which 'performance targets' are effected and reviewed.

Unit 17

PROMOTING YOUR COURSE

Every tutor, full- or part-time, has a vested interest in the continuation of his or her course. Professionally, of course, one's aspirations will be much higher than this crude baseline. One will be proud of and want actively to promote one's course, whether as tutor or as course leader. Hopefully, this view will be even more embracing: the wish to promote the college itself, of which one's own section is just a small part.

In Unit 10 we looked at college mission statements. In a very real sense all course promotion must begin from this important starting point: the overall intention of the institution. But, while the college as a whole may be more than the sum of its component parts, nevertheless these individual building blocks – and courses – are usually what account for local reputation. With respect to large institutions, at least, members of the public do not usually know about or discuss college successes, but rather the experiences of people they know who have, in their view, succeeded or failed because of specific course experiences. We have laboured this point because we believe that it is crucial at a very fundamental level to the health of an institution that every tutor feels a personal commitment, and that staff do not regard promotion of courses as a job for 'them out there' in some amorphous senior management or even marketing team.

Similarly, it would be most unwise to rely *solely* on attendance at a couple of annual careers conventions or similar events to promote one's course. Experience suggests that such events may have some public-relations value, but often they fail to deliver suitable potential students the following September. Task

60 in this Unit looks through brief cameos or descriptions of real incidents at such events, and at some of the failings of this kind of promotion. You may find it helpful to tackle this Task in order to clear away the negative aspects of promotion before looking more positively at the issues for the rest of the Unit.

Task 60   Looking at course promotion through careers conventions or similar events

Below are three cameos of actual events which took place at events designed to publicize college courses. Read each cameo in turn. In each case imagine you were the tutor involved. What would you have done?

Cameo 1   As course tutor you are asked to advertize your specific course at a careers convention in a local high school. You turn up, along with several students, and discover not only other professions represented (e.g. banking, the police, etc.,) but your own college's careers section, too. In the course of the day, unknown to you, some of the students visit their own college's careers stand and ask about entry to their own course. They are supplied with inaccurate information.

Cameo 2   As course tutor you are asked to attend a careers convention, and as usual you take along some students who are following your FE 16–19 course. During the day they visit a stand belonging to the local polytechnic, where they are advized that success in your course will gain them admission to a degree programme. You believe this to be untrue; but the hopes of several of them are raised and they fill in application forms. Two weeks later they receive rejection notices indicating that they will not have adequate entry qualifications at the end of the course.

Cameo 3   As course tutor you are asked to give a detailed explanatory talk about your course to a group of teachers and headteachers at a twilight session lasting two hours. You turn up well prepared and take a fellow tutor and some of your best advertizements: six students from the course. You discover that the event, in a very large hall with a lot of space, has attracted an audience of 200. Then the organizer emerges and objects to the attendance of the students and your colleague as they were not specifically invited!

We have begun this Unit with a few reflections on why individual tutors need to promote their own courses, and also with some cautionary tales about facile assumptions relating to promotion through the more obvious marketing ploys such as careers conventions, in order to set the scene for a more varied approach. We have also, so far, used the relatively neutral term 'promote', rather than 'market' or 'sell'; but it is worth discussing these latter descriptions briefly.

In recent years the political climate has promoted a market economy – even in education, which has always fought shy of this in the past. Many educationalists regard words culled from business and commerce as dirty; but, whatever one's view, the reality has to be faced that colleges have to attract students. For this reason we detect in some colleges an adoption of 'marketing' strategies (which are deemed respectable, and include college brochures, course literature, the appointment of marketing officers, etc.), rather than of 'selling' techniques. Selling suggests that a producer (the college) provides a product (a course) which is sellable to a customer (a student will sign up to attend). All the 'marketing' in the world will not help unless the final 'sale' is made, and students do turn up to study on your course. It may be too crude for some palates, but the fact is that colleges are indeed selling products to customers and must win sales to survive. We go on now to look at some ways in which this might be done with reasonable satisfaction for both the producers (you, your courses) and the customers (potential and actual students).

Here are some ways in which you can reach potential students:

- through individual links with school careers staff
- through the careers officers (who need reliable information from you)
- through attending careers conventions and similar events
- through fly-sheet adverts, e.g. in local libraries
- through newspaper adverts
- through use of newspapers to cover college/course events
- through college/faculty open days or evenings
- through mail-shots to selected groups
- through canvassing employers
- through special initiatives (e.g. setting up a caravan in the high street on a Saturday or handing out leaflets in the street)
- through distribution of course brochures and college literature in the local area.

In much of the above, what counts is the quality and clarity of the course information, and it is to this issue that we now invite you to turn your attention.

Compiling a course brochure

Before you set out to compile your course brochure you will need to address some quite fundamental questions. These are set out in Table 34.

TABLE 34 Compiling a course brochure

Question	Issues and examples
1 What is the audience for the brochure?	e.g. School students, adults – any specific sub-group, such as returners etc.
2 What are the messages you want to convey about the course?	e.g. Duration, level, employment opportunities, entry qualifications, work experience, assessment processes, etc.
3 What ethos do you want to convey about the course, and about college life and work?	This may be especially important to mature students. What about open learning, creche facilities, an equal opportunities policy statement?
4 How will the brochure be used?	e.g. Mail-shots may need a different approach from leaflets handed out at a careers convention.
5 What is the most appropriate language or style to use?	Accessibility is a key word.
6 What format will work best?	Design is important – see do/don't checklist.
7 Are there clear instructions for application?	Check for ambiguities.
8 Is there a contact point (name, address, phone no.) for information *before* clients become committed to applying?	Aways allow free access to course/students before they become committed.

Now that you have considered the *content* of your course leaflet, it is perhaps appropriate to examine in more detail some ideas for format. Here are some ideas to think about.

Don't	*Do*
• Use too much colour or it will distract the eye from the text	• Use colour, in moderation – two contrasting colours work best
• Provide too much detail of subject content	• Provide only the main areas of study
• Give an exhaustive list of jobs, including those with only	• Give a short list of possible careers to which the qualifica-

- remote interest to students gaining this qualification
- Leave out important course detail, e.g. work-experience arrangements

- Leave out entry requirements as this could lead to disappointment or delay in enrolling for a more suitable course
- Forget to cost out your leaflet.

- tion leads by way of a guideline
- Include information about work experience because students, in particular mature students, may need to make different child-care arrangements on these days if different hours are kept
- Include course entry requirements to encourage prospective students to aim for realistic goals
- Decide whether you want a modest in-house production, or a more polished product.

You have now thought through the purpose of course promotion, some questions about what exactly you wish to promote, the audience for the promotion, and some aspects of giving a format to your promotion. Attempt Task 61 below.

Task 61   Designing a course leaflet for your own course

Try to design (and, if appropriate, do actually produce) your own course promotion materials.

Dealing with applicants and applications

Let us now move on to assume that, following your promotion, a prospective student has filled in an application form, and appears on paper to have the necesssary qualifications, or hopes to gain them in forthcoming exams. He or she will then be invited along for an interview by you, the course tutor. (N.B. too, increasingly colleges are establishing Access Centres which will recommend students to a particular course on the basis of an assessment interview.) Application forms, in general, give you a reasonable idea of the student's previous education. Other relevant background information can be provided by the prospective student if the form is well designed to leave space for 'additional information' the student considers relevant to the application. To a large extent you may be bound by college application forms; but try to encourage prospective students to write relevant information about themselves in as much detail as possible.

Entrance tests

Courses not requiring examination success for entry will nevertheless need to devise a recruiting procedure, often including some form of assessment as well as an interview. An entrance test may be the answer. This will need to be tailored to meet the needs of the individual course concerned. For example, if course work or the career to which the course leads involves written reports of any kind, a possible entrance test could be a piece of written work, perhaps an essay on a theme, or a letter, or a simulated work activity. A live issue now is the accreditation of prior learning (APL). You will need to devise strategies for assessing the prior learning of potential students on both the practical and theoretical levels.

Planning the interview process

Successful interview procedures are never ad hoc, but are always planned by the team. Courses may have differing requirements, and there is no one format for interviewing. But there are a few ideas you might like to consider:

- Will prospective students meet existing students?
- Will they spend long enough in the college to gain a 'feel' for the institution?
- Will they have a fair chance to put *their* questions?
- Will they see their potential base or workrooms?
- Will they meet a cross-section of staff?
- Will they see, and be seen by, representatives of the employment sector they hope to join?

The interview

An interview is a two-way process which means that the interviewer needs to address two questions:

- Is the student right for this course?
- Is this course right for this student?

If a positive response to either of these central questions is in any doubt, possible alternative courses need to be recommended and career guidance given; or the student needs to be re-directed to other members of staff or a careers officer assigned to the college, for assistance.

Any other motive, other than those addressed by the two questions above, such as filling places on unpopular courses in order that they continue to run, or for financial reasons (if the course is a profitable one), is unethical and should never be given any consideration by an interviewer.

The interviewer

The ideal person for the job is one who *knows* the course and where it leads, however diverse the opportunities may be; otherwise students with ambition in particular directions may be wrongly advised. Course tutors therefore will usually be involved as interviewers, as they know the aims and objectives of their course, details of content and progression, and should know as far as it is possible all the relevant career possibilities available to the qualified student. Course tutors will often, however, share interviewing with other course staff so that they, too, can extend their skills, and so that they can feel committed to the students who are recruited.

Interview information

The information gleaned from an application form is not always adequate for a full assessment of a prospective student. It is advisable to ask interviewees to bring along their Records of Achievement, or references from employers of would-be mature students. Make this clear when the student is invited for interview.

First impressions

Prospective students will usually place a great deal of emphasis on the impression they create at interview. Of equal importance is the impression *you* create! To create a good impression every time you must always:

- Welcome the student in a warm, friendly way but not in a *totally* informal manner. Remember eye-contact.
- Be polite, even if the interviewee arrives late (although some explanation may be sought).
- Be well-informed about the course you run and be ready to answer any questions candidates may have; indeed, provide opportunities for any questions.
- Begin with a reasonable summary of the course – content, requirements in terms of qualifications, expectations in terms of effort and commitment, attendance on work placements and future employment opportunities/higher education opportunities.
- Remember that you *represent* your college each time you speak to a prospective student. Always aim to project a professional image, but one which is caring and sincere.
- Give a reasonable amount of time for the student to think and reflect.

- Always explain 'what happens next' to the students, their next 'move' and yours. They need to be informed of possible dates when you will contact them regarding a place on the course and if they need to supply any further information, e.g. exam results (a form could be supplied for this purpose).
- End the interview with friendly comments, thanking the interviewee for attending, etc.

The influence of personal bias

As an individual, you will already have an image of the ideal student for your course in your mind. This is usually made up of a collection of traits you expect your students to possess. This predetermined attitude will affect the *type* of questions you ask, and to *whom* – studies have shown that interviewers sometimes fail to pose key questions to certain students. You might do well to consider the traits you feel a member of the profession to which your students aspire will need to possess. You will also need to check your perceptions with those of your tutor colleagues, or you may use your consultative group for the course as a forum in which to debate the issue. This will help to broaden your view.

Compiling an interview form

You will make an even more fair and reasoned judgement if you complete an interview form for each prospective student. Such forms may serve as a basis of later discussion by the interviewers about which candidates should form the final selection. (It is also useful to have a reserve list lest any accepted candidates drop out later: reserves can be informed that they are on such a list.) The precise content of the interview form will differ from course to course and might be usefully discussed at course team meetings and reviewed after each batch of interviews.

Conclusion

This Unit has tried to present the promotion of college courses from the point of view of a course leader and of a course team member; but we have not forgotten the perspectives of existing students and, most important of all, of potential students. In this way the Unit has pursued a basic theme of the present book: the partnership of teachers and learners.

Unit 18

MANAGING TIME

Looking at your own time and its management

The effective professional is the one who manages his or her time well. So what is the skill of effective time management? To begin with, you can only begin to manage time when you have a clear idea about how you spend time now. Armed with this knowledge you can examine what is currently valuable, what activities can be speeded up or delegated, and what things can be abandoned or modified. So let us begin with the present.

The best place to start is for you to identify what you see as priorities in your workload.

Task 62   Identifying your own priorities for the use of time

1   What do you see as the priorities for your job? List them in rank order.
2   Now try to assess what percentage of a working week each of these priorities takes up. Put your estimates against each item on the list.
3   What are the problems you experience in trying to find time to pursue these priorities?

This brief stocktaking exercise should help you later when you come to look in detail at how you use your time. If Task 62 has identified some of your ideals or aspirations in time management then the next Task should explore the realities! You need to do some research on yourself and your workload, but to do it as objectively as possible. This is how it works:

▶ Task 63   Keeping a self-report time-log

1   Identify a period when you are prepared to allocate a few minutes each day to logging the jobs you actually do. Periods in mid-term are 'more typical', so avoid first and last weeks of term. Select a block of time, not less than two weeks and not more than four.
2   During the chosen block, use the guide in Table 35 to help you analyse your workload. Keep the appropriate records.
3   At the end of the block, analyse your use of time.
4   How does the reality of the chosen time-block compare to ideals you identified in Task 62? Where are the discrepancies and how do you account for them?

TABLE 35   A suggested format for keeping a time-log

(Use a proforma like this each day during the chosen time-block.)

Time period	Tasks undertaken	Who else involved
8.00–8.30		
8.30–9.00		
9.00–9.30		
etc.		

To analyse the log, assign each time-period to an appropriate heading. Devise your own headings to fit in with your specific job; the following are useful examples only:

* administration
* management
  – of people
  – of finance
  – of plant
* teaching
* curriculum development
* in-service activity
* committee membership
* chairing committees
* interviewing

- pastoral care
  - of students
  - of staff
- policy formulation, etc.

At this point you should have a fairly clear perception of how you spend time, and how that reality squares with your intentions about priorities. Using this data about yourself you may need to work out some strategies for bringing the two things closer together. The following questions may help:

- According to your priorities and the findings from your self-analysis research, what are you doing too much of?
- Can any of these things be abandoned? What would happen if they were?
- Can any of these things be delegated or shared in any way? What effect will this have on their time-management and workloads?
- Can any of these things be speeded up? Or can they be simplified?
- Can some less important jobs be re-scheduled in any way, so that they can be done at non-peak times when they produce fewer conflicts of time-demand?
- What are you doing too little of?
- Are there any ways of achieving identified priorities more quickly?
- Are there any strategies which would sustain priorities while cutting down on the time spent?
- Could your time-keeping systems be improved, e.g. the way you plan appointments or manage your administration?

Ways of managing time more effectively

The following are some ploys commonly used by managers to improve their efficiency in time management:

- prioritizing all jobs and completing them in strict order (with, of course, an eye to fixed deadlines)
- keeping checklists of tasks to be done each day
- for major activities, setting out a list of sub-tasks with individual deadlines
- making use of administrative staff to undertake appropriate tasks
- using a team and team roles effectively
- being realistic about what is achievable
- planning for the short, medium and long term, so that future goals are not lost sight of even when immediate issues intrude

- arranging the working day so that e.g. an intensive period can be spent on administrative tasks early/late in the day when interruptions are fewer
- not being a slave to the telephone such that each phone call is effectively promoted ahead of other priorities
- using quiet periods (pre- and post-term working days, for example) to clear any backlogs
- keeping meetings over which there is control to a sensible length, and keeping the agendas and discussion productive
- preparing in advance for all meetings so that they are businesslike
- learning basic time-saving techniques, e.g. rapid reading, use of a dictaphone, use of a word-processor
- being punctual and keeping others to time
- learning to say 'No' when appropriate
- keeping both a diary (for day-to-day organization) and a year-planner (to plan and ensure that the medium and long-term priorities are being addressed).

Earlier in this Unit you were asked to keep a log of your own use of time. In this section we are going to present some data from a similar log kept by an FE lecturer who was, at the time, both a head of department and the manager of an out-of-town multidisciplinary site. The data illustrates the kind of information which can be gathered from the kind of self-analytical record described in this Unit, and the uses to which it can be put.

Table 36 shows the analysed data collected in one week. Headings were devised to show the different categories of work undertaken, and the relative proportions of time spent on them.

The data needs to be viewed against pre-identified priorities which looked like this:

1   the smooth operation of courses at the delegated site with respect to both staff and students
2   the effective management of the head of department's own cluster of courses
3   high quality of teaching of students by self and others
4   some reorganization of departmental middle-management structures
5   curriculum review and strengthening in specific areas of the department.

What is clear from even a cursory glance at the self-analysis data compared to the articulated priorities is that there is a significant mismatch!

TABLE 36   Data on time spent by one FE Head of Department/site head in a case-studied week, analysed by category of task

Task	% of time
Departmental and site administration	44.7
Curriculum matters	17.5
Internal college committees	9.4
Teaching	6.2
Interviews with students	5.4
Interviews with staff	5.4
Liaison with external agencies	4.2
Departmental management functions	2.4
Reading and updating	2.4
Dealings with senior admin staff	1.2
Miscellaneous travel	1.2
TOTAL	100% = 41.8 hours

Note: The week chosen for the study turned out by chance to be 'untypical' in that it was a week without evening or Saturday teaching and with only one college-based committee meeting. Nevertheless, the total workload consumed 39% more time than the 'official' working week of 30 hours allowed.

Task 64   Assessing the mismatch between time usage and identified priorities

1   Do your own assessment of the mismatch between the data in Table 36 and the same lecturer's identified priorities.
2   Speculate about possible causes for the mismatch.

The lecturer concerned in the above research decided to explore the situation further by going back over all diaried commitments for a term. Each commitment was assigned to an appropriate category, and the relative proportions of each type of commitment were calculated. The results of this alternative form of time analysis are shown in Table 37.

Table 37 highlights the way in which committee meetings can dominate workload. The meetings concerned varied from two hours to three-and-a-quarter hours in duration, and most involved round-trip travelling of either half-an-hour or an hour.

TABLE 37   Analysis of diaried commitments for one Autumn Term for a FHE Head of Department/Site head

Type of commitment	No. of occurrences	% of total
College-based committee meetings	28	18.6
Meetings with department staff to discuss FE curriculum	16	10.6
Interviews WITH students	16	10.6
Interviews OF students	14	9.3
Meetings with individual dept/site staff	14	9.3
Liaison meetings with outside agencies	13	8.6
Teaching commitments	10	6.6
Interviews with potential staff	8	5.3
Meetings with academic staff – not dept or site, e.g. INSET officer	6	4.0
Dept management group meetings	5	3.3
Visits to principal or deputies	4	2.6
Attendance at external committees	4	2.6
Liaison with LEA advisers	4	2.6
Visits to main site, administration centre	4	2.6
Attendance at conference	3	2.0
External consultancy	1	0.7
College function (prize-giving)	1	0.7
TOTAL	151	100%

There were seventy working days in the term, which means that each day included, on average, 2.2 commitments of the kind listed in Table 37. Again, the research is helpful in highlighting an important time-management issue: the weighting of a senior manager's workload towards major commitments at the expense of less formal time for innovative activity.

The amounts of time spent on curriculum matters are, arguably, too small; and perhaps too little time was allocated to departmental, as opposed to site, management. Obviously, the data are open to interpretation; but hopefully, the small-scale research quoted nevertheless gives a flavour of how valuable such activity can be. The research could certainly be justified on a number of counts:

- First and foremost, the act of collating the data is valuable action-research and is, in its own right, an in-service exercise. In the present case it illuminated and quantified, to one manager, what was previously only impressionistic; and it allowed decisions to be made about priorities based on real information.

- Second, the collation process helped to raise an awareness of college-wide issues of management structure (such as the appropriateness of the departmental structure as a tool of management). These issues might, in the right circumstances, have been debated in a collegiate management forum, and action taken.
- Third, the research suggests a need for time-management training. Since so much of an individual's workload in the situation described was externally imposed, it was doubly critical that the management of time was well handled for the remaining slots. Overwork, too, is a significant issue, and one rarely addressed because it is valuable for institutional survival.
- Fourth, the research showed the centrality of two skills to managers: committee skills (both membership and chairmanship), and administrative (including financial) skills. Even the art of dealing with an in-tray is tackled without preparation by most beginning managers.
- Fifth, also high on the agenda is the ability to deal effectively with curriculum issues; but clearly a great deal of this work was delegated (to course tutors in this case). So, by implication, managers need to train, or ensure training for, delegated curriculum managers.
- Sixth, the analyses show up a list of other requisite management skills that would form part of an in-service agenda, for example:
  – interview skills with staff
  – interview skills with students
  – skills of liaison with external agencies, and so on.
- Finally, the research shows up in-service issues that need to be addressed because time for them is limited and they need to be handled efficiently. These are, perhaps, best presented as questions:
  1   How can time be found for reading and updating?
  2   How can management be combined effectively with a teaching role?
  3   How can time be found for the manager to pursue legitimate professional activities such as consultancies?
  4   Above all, how can managers be given time to *reflect* on the process of management with a view to self-improvement?

Action-research and the manager

Traditional management-training courses (such as current ones dealing with the Education Reform Act, or run by specialist consultancy companies) tend to focus on the manager's immediate need for knowledge (such as financial knowledge) or the theoretical constructs of management. Other approaches concentrate on psychological theory to influence 'people' skills, or attempt to set up management models based on specific sociological world-views.

In the practical world of FHE management, a more useful approach might be one which concentrates on job analysis. The data reported here were only a first step on this path for one such manager; but they may throw some light on the potential of the approach if vigorously pursued by, for example, all the managers in a single institution as part of an in-service exercise.

In an open institution where this kind of data could be discussed, one might go a step further. Each individual manager could supply case-study analysis of his or her own situation. Thus, in the present case much management time was consumed by committees: workload in this respect was replicated by that of peer-group managers. Suppose the null hypothesis were tested: most decisions of real importance to the college are not taken in committee meetings. Then, if the research showed that committees DID take the important decisions this would lend further weight to the suggested need for managers to be trained in committee skills. By contrast, the opposite finding (that important decisions were taken outside the committee structure) would call into serious question the use of managers' time in attending numerous long meetings. This kind of research has reality; but it is, of course, highly threat-laden because it questions conventional practice and college expectations.

In particular, the data reported here highlight the need for college principals to initiate, join in and be influenced by continuing management analysis of their institutions with a view to evolutionary change in the interests of increased efficiency and effectiveness. The larger the institution the more critical the need.

The next Unit goes on to look at another important aspect of management: the management of people.

Unit 19

LEADING STAFF TEAMS

'Management is tasks. Management is a discipline. But management is also people.'

Peter S. Drucker, 1977

Most readers of this book will have some management responsibilities: for example, for student learning or course design and delivery. But most full-time tutors will also manage people – as co-workers with part-time staff, or as course leaders or section leaders. Many will aspire to head a school, department or faculty. At whatever level the management responsibility, the same basic principles govern the leadership of staff teams.

Task 65   Analysing your leadership role

Think carefully about what you actually do:
- Are your functions common to *all* leaders of staff teams?
- If not, which are common to all team leaders?
- Consult your colleagues in the department and, if possible, one or two from another department.

Keep your findings as they will enable you to consider later on the influence they have on your leadership style.

Now that you have looked at your own specific situation you may care to reflect on the wider picture: the limitations placed upon you by college, local authority and national government policies. You are also constrained by the expectations society has of the service you offer, and you have to work within certain boundaries of authority, accountability and responsibility. The results of your work are also up for scrutiny at all times; therefore *your own ability to lead, motivate and control your team, within all these limiting factors,* is on show!

Some people believe, rather naively, that leadership is about power. Actually, it is about responsibility, and the ability to work within constraints. The diagram gives the flavour; but perhaps you could add to it, or draw your own. (Figure 4).

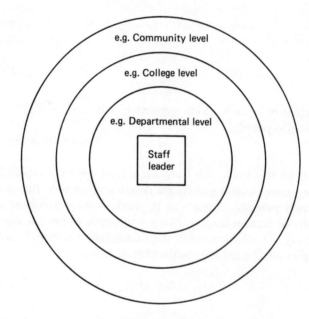

Figure 4   Influences and constraints on staff managers and leaders

People who lead teams in any job hope to be classed as a person with the two 'e's – effectiveness and efficiency. One key to possessing these two qualities lies in careful planning, long- and short-term. Thought and planning often take place away from the workplace; in the car, at home, mowing the lawn, even while washing the dishes. These thoughts and plans are essential (though we shall caution later in the chapter about too headlong implementation of them); so let us glance at what they might typically encompass for a course leader.

The planning process

As we have seen elsewhere in this volume good teaching depends upon good planning.

- The first thing you need to consider are the intentions for your course. As leader, you need to be clear where you are going and what is to be achieved.
- Aims and objectives follow, and are more specific to each element of the course.
- Resources (financial and material) need to be taken into account: those already available and those required.
- You need to make a mental inventory of the strengths, skills and limitations of team members. Course team members need to be employed in the best possible way for them, you and the course. If this is carried out effectively, staff will feel professionally fulfilled and are likely to communicate better with other team members and begin to share common values.
- You need to reflect on how this ethos you are beginning to create for your course will be communicated to the students.

Getting team planning started

Once you have done your own thinking you will need to involve members of the team. This requires some subtlety. If team members are simply presented with a series of *faits accomplis* they are likely to be viewed at best as a 'waste of time' by the members. The best set of aims and objectives will be those devised by *you and the team together*, democratically. That way, team members feel a collective ownership and responsibility for the course from the outset. This may require some of the most demanding skills of the leader: tact, patience and diplomacy.

A good leader will be consciously and by turns:

- receiving professional wisdom from team members and using it
- moving members, through an educative process, towards better collect-ive decisions
- gently, but positively, filtering out the unworkable or second-rate.

Involvement of team members in the planning stage ensures that all team members know exactly what the purpose of their course is and exactly what it is intended to achieve. If the objectives are clear, precise and shared, and there is a clear time-scale, the results should be higher team motivation, greater creativity, less conflict and more efficient use of time and energy. Individual style of neither leader nor members is cramped by this method of working, because *the results to be achieved*, not personalities, form the main focus. It is up to the individual member of staff to work towards the goal in his/her own way, using freedom within agreed limits. This way individual teachers can give their best and provide the students with variety in teaching and learning styles. Objectives need to be reviewed from time to time, however. Regular meetings must make provision for this, in order that a 'reminder' is given as to objectives which are to remain constant, and a 'review' takes place for those which require updating.

Decision-making

One of the critical roles of the team leader is that of decision-maker. Some leaders become anxious, even oppressed, by that role. At a recent conference for curriculum leaders, during a small group workshop, one newly-appointed leader asked:

'What happens if I get it wrong?'

In our view, decision-making should begin more positively than this! Very few people who have been selected to leadership positions because of their professional ability, who listen to colleagues (even if they are not then swayed), and who have a few ounces of common sense and maturity, will make decisions so catastrophic as to be on their way to dishonourable discharge or even just an early pension. Making decisions is a part of everyday life and certainly forms an important part of college life. As team leader, you will need to make many decisions and one of these will be to decide who shares or even makes the decisions!

 ## Task 66   Deciding who makes decisions

Consider the following six tasks about which a decision needs to be made. Decide which members of your team would be involved in making the decisions and what degree of responsibility each would have.

- devising a new student pastoral support system for your course, to include tutorials
- drawing up a timetable for student assignment deadlines for this term
- implementing a new health and safety policy

- arranging placement visits for the students
- drawing up an agenda for the next team meeting
- choosing new floor-covering for one of the practical work rooms.

You will note how you use different people for different types of decisions. Some decisions involve more people: they are 'person-centred', others are more 'task-orientated'. Thinking about tasks in this way helps you to decide whether the right people are making the right decisions at the right level, because some decisions need to be implemented (as in the health and safety policy) whether staff agree with their introduction or not and are therefore task-orientated.

Delegation

Delegation is a much maligned word, usually associated with a team leader off-loading work. This is not the purpose of delegation. The concept is debased by the activities of some holders of leadership roles who reject responsibility in favour of power or, worse still, privilege. One middle manager we observed frequently requested to be accorded a title such as deputy head of department. Yet, whenever he was given a task to do, he contrived to divide it into sub-tasks which were passed on to main grade tutors to complete. Their collected work was then presented as the middle manager's own. This example epitomizes precisely what delegation is not! Rather, delegation is about prioritizing tasks, or choosing individuals with appropriate skills to carry out tasks on behalf of the team. One purpose of this delegation is to free the team leader for other, more pressing, roles.

Some team leaders are loath to delegate due to feelings of threat or loss of power. Others don't feel confident in the ability of their team members. There are risks, but these are usually outweighed by the success of delegation and team members usually welcome new opportunities if they are genuinely offered.

Occasionally, it does prove genuinely impossible to delegate. In those circumstances the first action is to analyse where the problem lies; the second is to pursue solutions with the college's senior management, since they will almost certainly have staffing or training implications outside the sole control of the team leader.

Relationships, communication and the leader

Earlier in this Unit, it was suggested that good leaders are both effective and efficient. Effectiveness and efficiency depend largely on staff morale, and when good working relationships break down, morale plummets!

Relationships depend on communication; if this is poor in a team, then relationships will suffer and so will the work of the team.

Leaders can take positive steps towards improving communication which will help anticipate and address problems. There are two possible approaches you might try; 'seeking', for problem-centred behaviour, or 'giving', for solution-centred behaviour.

'Seeking' behaviour looks for a positive response by focusing on the problems by:

- *reflecting* – 'bouncing back' ideas to prompt the other person to respond in more detail and allowing them to control the communications
- *inviting* – asking for suggestions, reactions, more information
- *clarifying* – asking for a check on understanding by the group of what has already been said.

'Giving' behaviour looks for an answer to the problem by directing – giving orders or instructions:

- *prescribing* – suggesting what could be done
- *challenging* – blocking, or criticizing what has been said
- *negotiating* – offering a bargain or trade-off.

Where possible, 'seeking' behaviour is likely to be more effective than 'giving' behaviour, though there are occasions when the latter becomes inevitable. However, this may be less true where the leader possesses listening skills. This is something which needs to be encouraged amongst all team members. As team leader you need to consider the following points regarding the development of *your own* listening skills:

- Aim to concentrate on what the other person is saying and not on what you want to say next.
- Aim to listen to *everything*, not just parts of the sentence you want to hear!
- Aim to ignore all distractions, other people talking, the telephone, etc.
- Aim to listen with an open mind, not one that is already made up.
- Aim to follow this by questions totally relevant to what was said.

The contrast between the 'seeking' style of leadership and the 'giving' style, and the tension between them, are illustrated neatly in Figure 5.

The 'Johari window' is another useful model through which you can examine the way you, as a leader, control the flow of information through the team, as well as to and from your Senior Management Team. It looks at the way and extent to which you are prepared to show your feelings and opinions,

Figure 5   Leadership styles: seeking and giving

and the extent to which you gain information from other people about how they see your behaviour: the feedback. Task 67 uses an adaptation of the Johari model.

To look through the Johari window at yourself and your own style of leadership behaviour you need to proceed to the next task.

Task 67   Examining your own leadership

Consider the eight situations which follow. You need to decide which course of action you would take in each case (a, b or c). It might help to reflect on any similar, real situations you have been involved in and what you did at the time. Above all, be honest: there are no 'correct' answers, and no-one to cheat but yourself!

I   Your head of department has gone 'over your head' and assigned an important project to one of your team. Would you:
   (a)   tell him/her politely that he/she is undermining your authority?
   (b)   ask him/her how he/she feels about the way you handle such projects?
   (c)   say nothing and try and maintain good relations with your head of department?

2   Your head of department and another departmental head were holding a conversation when you entered the room. The other head of department had just 'let slip' a new plan that you didn't know about which would damage your promotion prospects. Would you:
   (a)   explain how you feel about it?
   (b)   ask for further information about the plan?
   (c)   leave it until your boss told you about it?

3   During a discussion with a team member 'DCF' is mentioned (discounted cash flow). You know nothing about it. Do you:
   (a)   admit you know nothing about it?
   (b)   ask for an explanation?
   (c)   change the subject?

4   You appear to have a 'personality clash' with a member of your team which makes working together very difficult. Do you:
   (a)   'clear the air' – bring your feelings out into the open?
   (b)   ask your colleague to talk the issue through?
   (c)   say nothing, try to be businesslike in your dealings with your colleague?

5   You have just heard a dreadful rumour about a team member's personal life. Would you:
   (a)   tell him all you know?
   (b)   tactfully ask if he/she is ok?
   (c)   pretend to know nothing and say nothing?

6   A member of your team has submitted a report which is very critical of the performance of your team to your head of department. Would you:
   (a)   tell him/her you feel hurt by this action?
   (b)   ask him/her how you could all improve the team effort?
   (c)   say nothing, but keep it in mind for future reference and revenge?

7   In conversation with your head of department, 'NVQ' (national vocational qualifications) was mentioned in relation to the standard of your course. You are asked about its 'position' on 'the ladder', but are unsure of the precise details. Do you:
   (a)   admit your lack of precise knowledge?
   (b)   ask for clarification?
   (c)   change the subject?

8   You have recently suffered from personal problems and have been irritable at work. A team member has commented how you can't be relied on for help at the moment. Do you:

(a)   apologize and tell him/her about your problems?
(b)   ask what you have been doing wrong?
(c)   try to help with this problem and avoid the personal aspects?

Now look at your answers; the number of times you chose 'a' shows the extent to which you are prepared to disclose your attitudes and views. The 'b' answers show the extent to which you look for feedback from other people and the 'c' answers show no communication with other people at all.

You can record your score on the 'window' in Figure 6. Draw a horizontal line across from the number representing the number of 'a's you ticked. Draw a vertical line up from the number representing the total times you ticked 'b'.

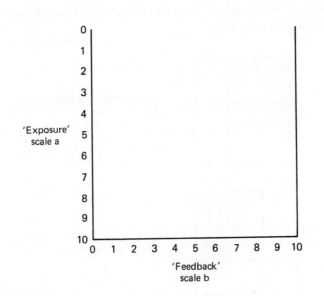

Figure 6   Your own Johari window

The 'shape' of the window in the box in Figure 6 can now be compared with that in Figure 7 for the purposes of commentary and interpretation.
The window has four sections and two axes (Figure 7). The axes represent exposure and feedback.
The Arena indicates how much of a situation tends to be known to you and to others involved.
The Blindspot represents things others know about but you don't.
The Facade is what you show to others.
The Unknown are things unknown to you and others.

	Arena	Blindspot
Exposure	Façade	Unknown

Feedback

Figure 7   The Johari window explained (Luft and Ingham 1969)

► Task 68   Analysing your leadership style

Compare your 'window' shape with those in Figure 8 and the explanations. What have you learned about yourself?

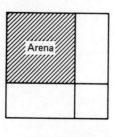

An enlarged arena shows an effective style of interpersonal relations.

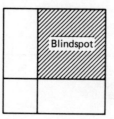

An autocratic leadership style leads to a large blindspot.

Figure 8   Analysis of Johari windows

Think about how the window shows your ability to communicate openly and how this can affect your performance as team leader.

Improving your performance as a team leader

The last exercise will have shown how you are open to the influence of your team or otherwise. In order to improve your performance you need to consider in which direction you need to move, i.e. involve team members *more* or *less* in decision-making and implementation of the task. It can be seen that in doing so, three concerns are paramount:

- achieving the tasks and seeing that short- and long-term plans are carried out
- building and reinforcing the needs of the group for teamwork and team spirit
- meeting individual needs of every team member in order that they reach full potential.

Figure 9   Aspects of leadership

John Adair (1985) sees these three aspects as overlapping circles, as in Figure 9. If the task achievement circle is neglected, so are parts of the group and individual circles, for lack of attention to the task causes disruption to the group and dissatisfaction to the individual. On the other hand, achievement of objectives is needed for group and individual morale to be high. If the team circle is neglected the other two aspects are again affected. The team leader must see that the needs of the group are met, otherwise little can be achieved. If individual needs aren't met, then team and task needs will suffer accordingly. It can be seen that all three circles represent *equally* important aspects of management which are mutually dependent.

Let us take a closer look at each of the three aspects in turn:

Achieving the task

As team leader you need to:

- make a workable plan
- brief the team carefully on the task and plan
- delegate tasks to team members
- keep overall control of the task implementation by regular meetings

- speed up/slow down implementation as necessary
- give policy reminders when applicable.

Building the team

As team leader you need to:

- set and maintain team standards
- encourage team effort
- support by relieving tension with humour
- keep a check on disruptive individuals
- assess team performance
- assist the team with group appraisal of its own performance.

Developing Individuals

As team leader you need to:

- find out about any special skills or knowledge individuals have which are relevant to the task
- encourage individual contributions and deploy them
- 'sort out' disagreements between individuals by discussion
- make sure every team member takes part and makes his/her best effort.

It is also your responsibility as leader to help team members with their own professional self-development. You should make time available to counsel individuals on personal-relationship issues. Finally, each team member should be helped to write a personal development plan which should be reviewed every few months, as planned development leads to a feeling of being valued and greater self-esteem. The team also benefits as a whole, as the overall effectiveness of the team increases because of the increase in combined skills. Not only this, but with increased individual awareness, the team becomes more supportive, and morale improves. This will become increasingly important as schemes of appraisal are adopted.

▶ Task 69   Sharing your thoughts on your own leadership

(This is a task for the very brave only.) Discuss with a trusted team member his or her view of your leadership approach and see how it compares with your idea of yourself.

You may find the diagram in Figure 10 helps you and your colleagues share information.

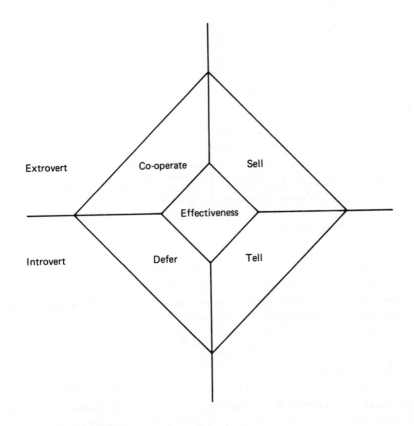

Figure 10   Leadership approaches

Time and the leader

As time passes you will gain in confidence and judgement as a leader, in turn inspiring greater confidence in your team. This is nicely illustrated in Figure 11.

Confidence-building with your team will be enhanced by some simple strategies:

- *Supporting* all the team members and encouraging them to support each other, especially when they make mistakes. Strengths and weaknesses are inevitable and these need to be recognized and addressed.
- *Co-operating* as a team means that collective needs will come before individual needs; working together can build trust in each other which means that team members are more likely to share ideas.

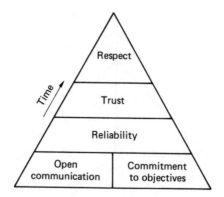

Figure 11   The leadership pyramid

- *Discussing* problems as a team keeps the team actively involved in progression and not regression. Always end discussion on a positive note for the future so that something constructive comes out of what could have started as a destructive comment.

Team meetings

Encouraging and providing a forum for discussion and contributions from your team may be facilitated by holding regular team meetings.

Team meetings need to be arranged systematically at intervals throughout the term. Regular meetings are useful for many reasons, but chiefly for updates on short- and long-term plans. If you set out clear aims and objectives, your meetings will have a ready-made agenda to start with – have the projected results been achieved? Regular meetings are also useful as a forum in which decision-making can be done in a democratic way. Problems can be dealt with more quickly and effectively if they require a consensus vote at these meetings.

Commitment to the team, too, is reinforced by regular meetings, and of course relationships are improved by the support given by other course members for new ideas. You will also gain valuable experience which will help develop your leadership skills by feedback from team members. Team identity can be strengthened by the following simple means:

- holding regular meetings which are friendly and productive
- identifying with a team name – it gives a common purpose
- having clearly defined roles within the team
- keeping the composition of the team stable, if possible
- leaving scope for individual talents to develop

- encouraging communication and sharing of ideas
- being aware of negative relationships within the group
- being aware of conflicting loyalties to other groups.

Conclusion

This Unit, though substantial, has done little more than scratch the surface of leadership in a college context. We have ignored some major issues such as:

- relationships between different teams, e.g. within a faculty or department
- what happens when outside pressures (e.g. new legislation or demands of a validating body) affect the team
- broader issues of sustaining morale and providing professional development
- what happens when one or more team members set out to be intentionally unhelpful or worse.

Some of the themes are discussed in other Units. Some are best left for more advanced training. However, the advice given here will see you through most of your early staff-leadership situations.

Task 70   Carrying out a final self-analysis

Finally, check through the following list (from Woodcock 1979) and see how many of these traits you possess, and how many you would hope to develop.

The successful team leader should:
1   be authentic and true to himself/herself and his/her own beliefs
2   use delegation as an aid to achievement and development
3   be clear about standards he/she wishes to achieve
4   be willing and able to give and receive trust and loyalty
5   have the personal strength to maintain the integrity and position of his/her team
6   be receptive to people's hopes, needs and dignity
7   encourage personal and team development
8   face facts honestly and squarely
9   establish and maintain sound working procedures
10   try to make work a happy and rewarding place.

Unit 20

SUSTAINING PERSONAL PROFESSIONAL DEVELOPMENT

Sustaining professional impetus

The biggest single problem for every teacher is to remain fresh, invigorated and dynamic. Only the continuous renewing of one's professional knowledge, skills and commitment will make this a reality. The whole of this book has been about honing professional skill through self-analysis of performance. Some might argue that this is the best and most effective form of professional development; and it has a good record of success. But there are other kinds of professional development which FE tutors will wish, or will be required, to undertake:

- staff meetings at course/department/faculty level
- college-run and in-house training on specific issues
- LEA courses, e.g. those run by advisory staff
- regional or national meetings of subject tutors
- courses put on by local providers, e.g. Professional Development Centre
- secondments to industry or commerce
- national courses and conferences, e.g. those by HMI
- Further Education Staff College events
- meetings of professional bodies
- externally validated taught qualifications – diplomas, degrees, etc.
- externally validated research qualifications
- professional qualifications relating to a vocational area.

Nowadays, many colleges and LEAs require staff to keep a record or inventory of their professional development, but the process is not universal. It is, however, valuable for every tutor to keep, at the very least, a personal log of the in-service work he or she has undertaken. This kind of log is increasingly being used in appraisal schemes; and it is a feature of some management training schemes as well. Nevertheless, though valuable, there are dangers in a bald list of courses attended or activities undertaken. The list does not give a rationale as to why those specific events have been chosen; nor does it provide an action plan for one's personal professional development. For this reason, it is suggested that it might be worth attempting a personal inventory updated at regular intervals, using the kind of format shown in Table 38. Alternatively, if your college has a format of its own, you may care to use that.

Task 71   Drawing up a personal professional development plan.

Carry out ONE of the following tasks.

EITHER
1   Use the proforma in Table 38 to assess your own recent and planned professional development.
OR
2   (a) Compare the proforma in Table 38 with a scheme for inventorying professional development which is used in your college. Add anything worthwhile to your existing scheme; then (b) Use the (augmented) inventory to assess your own recent and planned professional development.

Task 72   Discussing your training needs with your line manager

Since no personal development plan is of any value until it is operationalized, ask to discuss your plan with your line manager to gain his/her perceptions of it. Modify the plan if necessary. This may already be a part of your college's appraisal system.

Self-analysis in professional development

Central to this book is the notion that the professional should be the controller of his/her own learning destiny. This does not mean that a college cannot and

TABLE 38   A personal professional development inventory

1   Begin by listing all the professional development activities you have attended within, say, the last two or three years. Pay particular attention to
   - faculty training days
   - college in-house training
   - LEA courses
   - regional or national conferences
   - taught courses leading to qualifications
   - courses leading to research qualifications
   - update courses/secondments in your vocational area.

2   You may now begin to find patterns emerging, and it should be possible to break down the list into sub-groups of activities, e.g. those covering
   - administrative, financial and management skills
   - classroom-teaching skills
   - curriculum skills
   - vocational and workplace skills.

Look for the patterns, and subdivide your list.

3   Now review the value of the experiences. It might be helpful to use a page divided into columns, with headings such as those listed below:

Activity/event   Reason for attending   Quality/usefulness of the relevance to personal professional development

4   So far the inventory has looked back over the recent past. Using this stocktaking exercise, try to write a short assessment (possibly in list form as shown) of your current and future training needs:

Needs   Why you have this need
1
2
3

5   Finally, you will be able – in the light of this audit of needs – to be able to put together a training plan for yourself. Draw up a training plan which you would like to follow over the next two to three years (subject to later amendment, since circumstances do alter within that time span). Remember, your plan should be:
   - honest about your own needs
   - realistic about time-scales
   - achievable within known institutional/personal constraints
   - balanced between academic, pedagogic and vocational considerations.

should not require some kinds of professional development to be undertaken by its employees to meet institutional and authority needs: indeed, they must make such requirements. But it does acknowledge that it is the individual who should hold a conscious stake in his or her own learning. One of the most effective ways of achieving this is to come to understand and accept that *every situation is a learning situation*.

It is worth pausing to develop this point. Every tutor will be required over a term or a year to carry out certain professional tasks. These tasks, properly approached, well planned and effectively executed, will each be a source of professional development. Curriculum development is a common activity for tutors: indeed, syllabus or course requirements sometimes seem to change annually. But though rapid change is sometimes viewed as an irritant or a source of insecurity, the positive aspect of it is that it requires tutors to reassess and refine their work. A good professional attitude turns these 'irritants' into opportunities.

Closely related to curriculum innovation is the production of course documents. Happily, very few courses can survive now without good documentation which sets out, for example, the rationale of the course, its aims, teaching methods, content, assessment procedures and procedures for monitoring and evaluation. There was a time when this kind of documentation was not universally available; and the information was not communicated to students! But, actually, the process of compiling this kind of course documentation forces all of us as tutors to identify and articulate what we are about, and keeps us all up to the mark in delivering it. So, again, it is both a yardstick and a means by which professional development can take place. If the process of compiling course documentation is shared at course and department/faculty level, and if a proper academic and pedagogical debate ensues, then the learning process is further enhanced by the pooling of professional wisdom.

Other frequent events in the lives of FE tutors also provide opportunities for learning and professional development. Some typical situations can be regularly turned to advantage by reflecting on one's own performance, in

- experimenting with unfamiliar teaching methods
- helping students to learn from the workplace
- setting up a new base-room
- finding new work placements
- administering new processes, e.g. Records of Achievement
- managing new situations
- learning new curriculum material
- absorbing government circulars or information from professional bodies
- chairing consultative groups
- writing annual reports.

Perhaps a question in the reader's mind at this point is how best to utilize these situations. One technique is to keep a file of all the innovatory paperwork one creates so that, at a later date, the thinking processes can be traced, for example, during appraisal. In the cut and thrust of a busy professional life it is all too easy to neglect reflection in the cause of immediacy. Another useful professional activity is to keep a diary of key professional events with brief headings about the salient things one has learned through them. This does not have to be more than the 'Sunday' space, for example, in a modest academic year diary; though it could be in a separate log or even in a Filofax or one of its derivatives. Remember, though, the more cumbersome the system the more time it will consume and the less likely you are to sustain it. Elsewhere in this book we have included an example of how analysis of diary data can help the process of reflecting on management skills (Unit 14).

Task 73   Keeping a professional development diary

I   Adopt the suggestion of keeping a professional development diary. In addition to normal engagements, record examples of professional learning gained – especially those from day-to-day teaching and administrative events. Keep the recording system simple (e.g. headings and numbered points in your normal work diary).

2   Keep up the recording process for a reasonable period, perhaps six to twelve months as a minimum.

3   Look back over the diary. Does it
   • record evidence of professional development?
   • provide some starting points for further thinking about your own teaching and professional activity?

4   If the diary has proved useful, resolve to keep it going. Adapt the recording process in any way that you feel will prove more efficient or informative.

Some additional strategies for professional self-development

So far in this Unit three very significant points have been made. First, the need for all tutors to remain fresh and dynamic has been emphasized; after all, it may be your sixth time round teaching this course, but it is the first and only chance for the student to access it. Second, the most effective strategies for professional development put the tutor him/herself at the centre of the process. Third, the tutor's central role in self-development means that much of the learning takes place through self-identification of need, self-analysis of performance, and personal reflection on experience. With these principles established it may be helpful to look briefly at some more strategies that help the process of professional self-development.

One difficulty all tutors face is that of having to teach the same or very similar material more than once. Experience suggests that one is often most effective the first or second time of teaching any individual topic. So, a good ploy for staying fresh and developing one's own repertoire is to aim to teach any given topic differently on each occasion, if possible, and certainly not to regurgitate old lesson-notes. Thinking out new approaches can be more time-consuming but keeps alive a degree of challenge. In practice, too, each audience or class will be different and have slightly different needs; so this tactic is appropriate.

Time is a great pressure, and we all neglect important things like reading. It is helpful to find some time, however little, in which to read and update one's thinking. Even only one day in a term, though brief, can be extremely productive. A good ploy is to go to a suitable library for a day and look over all the back numbers of the journals relating to your teaching areas. A combination of brief notes and some photocopies will arm you with a lot of good, recent information in a short time.

Another valuable strategy is to dedicate just one week of the annual vacation period to a specific job: rewriting a curriculum document, composing an article, planning some classroom research, visiting a commercial or industrial site. Having done this, ensure that you take some vacation.

Getting the most out of in-service training

In this Unit the centrality of the tutor to his/her own professional development in the everyday work situation has been argued and illustrated. But some of that development also will be delivered through in-service training activities or courses. Part of the skill of self-development lies in learning to be analytical about the quality of these activities and in being able to learn from them. It is worth pausing, therefore, to consider some in-service training which you yourself have experienced.

Task 74   Analysing the value of in-service activities

1   Think of an INSET activity you have attended and enjoyed. Jot down three things that epitomize what was *good* about it.

2   Think of a poor piece of INSET which you have endured. Jot down three
     things that epitomize what was *bad* about it.

When you have completed Task 74 you will, in effect, have started to make
two lists. One will consist of things that motivate tutors on in-service work; the
second will be a list of de-motivators. You might like to compare your
responses with the lists in Table 39.
     To some extent the benefit an individual tutor can gain from a professional
development or in-service activity depends on the tutor's own approach and
discernment: one can even learn a great deal from negative experiences! But to
an extent, too, the level of professional development tutors can achieve can be
greatly enhanced if the preconditions within the tutor's institution are favour-

---

TABLE 39 Motivating and de-motivating factors in in-service work

Motivators

- Enjoyment
- Stimulation
- New knowledge gained
- New skills acquired
- Confidence boosted
- Increased level of personal performance
- Co-operative working with peers
- New qualifications gained
-
- (add your own items to this list)
-

De-motivators

- Activity difficult to access
- Activity in the wrong place
- Activity at the wrong time
- Activity at the wrong level
- Activity expensive on time
- Activity disruptive of private life
- Activity poorly delivered
- Activity in inappropriate learning style
- Course was unreasonable
- Course staff unsuitable
- No follow-up opportunity back in college
-
- (add your own items to the list)
-

able. The following list suggests some of the things that the managers of an institution can do in order to promote staff benefit from in-service training:

- create a climate in which personal professional development is regarded as the norm
- institute an effective needs-identification system
- ensure that those who receive training can put it to positive use
- plan and promote training so that it meets the needs of the individual, the college and the LEA
- show positive value of tutors' initiatives, research and other professional activities
- stimulate a positive view of change
- turn these attitudes and values into articulated policy
- make sure that not only staff and managers, but LEA officers, governors, etc. are aware of the policy.

Only within a fully supportive institutional framework can real professional development flourish. Too often one meets negative attitudes: a principal who believes that a tutor who writes a book must be selling college-time short, or a governor who thinks going to a national conference or carrying out classroom-based research is an excuse for not doing 'real work'. In fact, staff have a right to expect managers to be motivators of professional development by:

- acting as leaders
- providing reasonable resources
- linking with outside agencies
- being informed (about what is available for in-service training and about what staff are doing)
- acting as consultants and catalysts
- generating collaborative policies and, not least,
- setting an example.

In this section we have looked at getting the most out of in-service training and there has been an emphasis on motivation. In trying to sum up this process one is tempted to use a phrase such as: 'the best motivation of all is success.' Certainly we all need to succeed; and a new skill, a fresh insight, an additional qualification all help. But perhaps a more accurate summary would return to an earlier theme in this Unit:

'The best motivator of all is myself.'

Career planning

The remaining section of this Unit moves on from personal professional development to cast a quick glance at development within the context of the individual's career. Hopefully, the flavour of much of this Unit will have been that personal professional development has intrinsic value because of the improvement it will bring about in the tutor. It also has extrinsic worth because it ensures that students receive improved tuition. But it would be wrong to assume that tutors should not aspire to improved professional opportunities as a result of their enhanced skills: everyone needs the specific challenge of a new role, of promotion and of all that goes with these things. For this reason, tutors should not approach training just as an end in itself but can quite justifiably aspire to advancement through improved performance. So career planning is a valid part of a tutor's attempt to identify and meet training needs. This may best be exemplified through some brief case studies.

Case study 1: Jim   Jim is a part-time tutor in sociology. He is conscientious and liked by students. He has a first degree but not teaching qualifications. Jim would like to obtain a full-time post. He feels he has to prove his worth as a classroom teacher, but is worried that, at interview, he may be up against better-qualified candidates for the full-time posts. His dilemma is whether to take a course of initial teacher training (Cert.Ed.(FE)); to read for an M.Sc. in a specialist branch of sociology – social theory, or criminology perhaps – or to concentrate on going to short courses and on improving the college's existing curriculum materials on sociology.

Case study 2: Margaret   Margaret is a very able and energetic full-time lecturer, now course tutor. She has good exam results, and an excellent reputation in the region. In career terms she would like to progress to senior lecturer. She feels that her options include: taking a master's degree and moving to a college where she can do more advanced level work; alternatively she could stay put but try to volunteer for management activities in the faculty, and back up this experience by studying for a diploma in management studies.

Case study 3: Gill   Gill is a senior lecturer with a good track-record as a course tutor and a YTS organizer, and she has counselling experience. She has work-related qualifications, a master's degree and initial teach-training qualifications. She aspires to a post at deputy principal level. She feels that she should move towards strengthening her management claims through management training and is trying to decide between an MBA part-time or a period of secondment to gain experience of industrial management.

You might like to think out what advice would you give to Jim, Margaret and Gill. Then, if we were to add one further piece of background information about each of these tutors:

Jim   is an uninspired classroom teacher

Margaret   on a personal level, needs to be liked and finds it difficult to handle conflict situations

Gill   believes that women in management are most likely to succeed in pastoral posts, but would prefer to be a finance/resource manager,

would you now amend your advice? How? What *else* would you need to know before you could give genuinely helpful guidance to these tutors?

It is often easier to help others than oneself. But, finally in this Unit, it is time to take stock of your own career aspirations and the implications these have for your personal professional development.

Task 75   Assessing your own career aspirations

1   Take stock of your own career situation: where you are now, and what you would like to be doing in two, three or five years' time. Try to identify what you would like to be your next career move, and possibly the one beyond that. (N.B. Career moves may, of course, involve sideways moves to achieve long-term goals, not just promotion through the lecturer grading structure.)
2   What professional development would you need to achieve these goals?
3   Look back to the plans you made in Tasks 71 and 72. Do these need amendment?
4   Repeat this exercise every six months or so to take account of changing situations.

Unit 21

POSTSCRIPT

As this book goes to print, Further Education colleges and Local Education Authorities have just received copies of the Government's White Paper 'Education and Training for the 21st Century' (1991). This will effectively remove colleges from Local Authority Control and give them increased autonomy. The corollary of this is that colleges will have to become more responsive to the marketplace, more customer-orientated, and more quality-conscious. At the root of all quality in education is the fundamental quality of the classroom process – whether students learn effectively, whether they enjoy learning and whether teachers become experts at their craft. Although the White Paper puts much stress on the importance of college management, the ultimate quality of an educational institution will be found in its teaching and learning. This book is a contribution to that search for quality in the classroom process.

REFERENCES AND FURTHER READING

Adair J 1987 *Not bosses but leaders*
Kogan Page

Adair J 1988 *Developing leaders: Ten key principles*
Talbot Adair/McGraw Hill

Audit Commission 1985 *Obtaining better value from further education*
London: HMSO

Birch D 1988 *Managing resources in further education: a handbook for college managers*
Bristol: FESC

Davies P, Scribbins K 1985 *Marketing further and higher education*
York: Longman, FEU/FESC

Dean A, Heggarty S 1984 *Learning for independence*
London: FEU

DES 1987 *Non-advanced further education in practice: an HMI survey*
London: HMSO

DES 1990 *Work-based learning in further education: a review by HMI*
London: HMSO

DES 1991 *Education and training for the 21st Century*
London: HMSO

FESC 1989 *Work-based learning terms*
Bristol: FESC/Training Agency

FEU 1987 *Planning staff development: a guide for managers*
London: FEU

FEU 1988a *Planning the further education curriculum*
London: FEU

FEU 1988b *Staff development for a multicultural society*
London: FEU

FEU 1989a *Towards an educational audit*
London: FEU

FEU 1989b *The strategic planning of further education*
London: FEU

FEU 1989c *Women in post-16 education in Wales*
London: FEU (July 1989)

FEU 1989d *Anti-racist strategies in college and community*
London: FEU (September 1989)

FEU 1990a *Training for the future*
London: FEU/Training Agency

FEU 1990b *YTS: curriculum development through modular credit accumulation*
London: FEU

Haffenden I, Brown A 1989 *Implications of competence-based curricula*
London: FEU

HMI 1987 *Non-advanced further education in practice*
London: HMSO

HMI 1990 *Education observed: work-based learning in FE*
London: HMSO

Jessup G 1990a *Common learning outcomes: core skills in A/AS levels and NVQs*
NCVQ R and D Report no. 6

Jessup G 1990b *Accreditation of prior learning in the context of NVQ*
NCVQ R and D Report no. 7

Kerry T 1983 *Effective questioning*
Basingstoke: Macmillan

Luft J and Ingham H 1969 *Of Human Interaction*
California: National Press

National Council for Vocational Qualifications 1990 *NCVQ: a brief guide*
London: HMSO

NCC 1990 *Core skills 16–19: a response to the Secretary of State*
York: NCC

Sammonds P and Newbury K 1989 *Ethnic minorities in further and higher education*
London: ILEA/FEU

SCIA 1989 *Performance indicators in perspective: SCIA discussion paper no. 2*

Segal S 1984 *Society and mental handicap*
Tunbridge Wells: Costello Educational

Shukla K et al 1989 *Mainstream curricula in a multicultural society*
London: FEU

Training Agency 1990 *Act together: practical ideas and initiatives on youth learning*
Sheffield: Training Agency

TVEI 1990a *Choices for the future, no. 3: lectures in further education*
Bristol: TVEI

TVEI 1990b *Choices for the future, no. 4: curriculum managers in further education colleges*
Bristol: TVEI
TVEI 1990c *Developments in careers education and guidance*
Bristol: TVEI

TVEI and Careers Service 1991 *Post-16 work-based activities: a coordinator's guide*
Norfolk: Norfolk Educational Press

Warwick J 1990 *Planning a human resource development through equal opportunities: a handbook*
London: FEU

Woodcock M 1986 *The unblocked manager*
Wildwood

Wragg E C 1981 *Class management and control*
Basingstoke: Macmillan

INDEX